NEW WRITING AND WRITERS 18

NEW WRITING AND WRITERS
18

by

Yves Bonnefoy, Copi, A.R. Lamb,
B.C. Leale, Harry Mulisch, Naiwu Osahon,
Calum Ross, Tibor Várady

JOHN CALDER · LONDON
RIVERRUN PRESS · NEW YORK

This collection first published in hardback and paperback editions in Great Britain, 1980, by John Calder (Publishers) Ltd.,
18 Brewer Street, London W1R 4AS
and in a hardback edition in the U.S.A., 1980 by
Humanities Press Inc.,
Atlantic Highlands, New Jersey 07716
and in a paperback edition in the U.S.A., 1980 by
Riverrun Press Inc.,
175 Fifth Avenue, New York City 10010

The publishers gratefully acknowledge financial assistance from The Arts Council of Great Britain.

British Library Cataloguing in Publication Data
  New writing and writers
  18
  I. English literature – 20th century
   820'.8'00912   PR1148   80–41346

ISBN 0 7145 3773 x Casebound
ISBN 0 7145 3774 8 Paperbound

Photoset in 11/11pt Baskerville by Specialised Offset Services Ltd., Liverpool
Printed and bound in Great Britain by Redwood Burn Ltd.,
Trowbridge & Esher

CONTENTS

LIST OF
ACKNOWLEDGEMENTS

Some of the poems by B.C. Leale have previously appeared in the following magazines: *Contemporary Quarterly, Dream Helmet, Jazz/Linguis, Kayak, La Crecelle Noire, Pacific Quarterly, Slow Dancer, Tribune* and *Vanessa*.

'Loaves' was first published by The Mandeville Press, 'Other Worlds' by The Many Press and 'Offer' by The Starwheel Press.

INTRODUCTION

New Writing and Writers 18, as in previous issues, deliberately juxtaposes different, often violently different, trends in modern writing to give a varied picture of what is going on internationally. This is more important than ever because English letters, and American writing as well, have become increasingly insular, and unaware and disinterested in what is happening in other languages and other cultures. One disadvantage of this is that anyone starting to write in English finds his horizon forshortened and if he is trying to avoid the currently fashionable formula, will only meet editorial indifference.

NWW 18 presents three British writers, two of them, A.R. Lamb (*NWW 13*) and B.C. Leale (*NWW 16*) having appeared in this series before, who are now writing outside the fashionable mainstream in an original and very personal way, while the third, Calum Ross, makes his literary debut here. Lamb is a surrealist, his work aptly catching the placid unreality and flowing style of dream; Leale uses great economy to combine words and image, is also outside the norms of current English poetry, but is now winning a following especially among poets; Calum Ross on the other hand, in this earthy Scottish description of a New Year booze-up and its aftermath, the culmination of a novel which we did not feel we could publish in its entirety, is a naturalist writer with a keen ear for speech and eye for character.

Of the three writers from Western Europe included in this volume, one can only stress their difference. Harry Mulisch, whose satirical parable about modern bureaucracy was a highlight of *NWW 17*, opens the volume with an instructive and reflective anecdote about Mach, whose name we associate with speed and sound. Copi, the

Argentinian enfant terrible of the French theatre and
literary scene, contributes two stories from the nightmare
fringe of reality, while Yves Bonnefoy, one of the major
French poets of the present day is represented by 16 poems
translated by Elsie MacGregor.

Naiwu Osahon brings a direct political freshness to his
poems, an awareness of the exploitation of his country and
people by white Europeans in the past and by large and
small exploiters, whatever their colour in the present. Like
Brecht his polemic is simple, direct and effective and
represents effectively the way Africans see their present
situation. The last and major contribution to this varied
anthology is an extraordinary full length novel from
Yugoslavia, written originally, not in one of the major
languages of that country, but in Hungarian, still the
language of a small minority, and it catches the essential
tone of the people's democracies of Eastern Europe where
everyday life, as much as marxist dialectical theory, must be
enthroned in protective verbiage of a bland bureaucratic
hue. This is perhaps the most difficult text in the volume for
the Western reader, because it incorporates different levels
of   satire,   description,   reportage   and   experimental
technique.   It   already   has   an   important   reputation
throughout all Eastern European countries, although in
most of them it can only have an underground existence. It
is subversive in the way that literature has always been
most effectively dangerous to the régime, through exposure
to ridicule. Shakespeare and Johnson, Molière and
Beaumarchais, Rabellais and Swift, Pope and Burns, and
more recently Büchner, Shaw, Kaiser, Waugh, Orwell and
Edward Bond have all in their way subverted authority by
ridicule, sometimes so gently that only the alerted reader
could see the joke and realise the implication. For many
years now the political joke has been not just an East
European tradition, but a safety valve, an escape and a
short cut to truths that could not be baldly stated. And
often this specialized, often-grim, humour has not been
capable of translation to Western society.

In 1975 the publishers of NWW published in Britain an
extraordinary *samizdat*, a banned Russian novel entitled
Nobody by Nikolai Bokov, whose name can now be given
since he emigrated to Paris. This satire on Russian life, in

spite of enthusiastic reviews, made little impact in Britain, but NWW has since included Bokov material in *NWW 13, 14* and *17*. The current volume once again sticks its neck out with 'The Secret of the Mouse-Grey Room', hilariously funny to an East European capable of seeing through the paraphernalia of committee meetings, recordings of same, idealogical discussions and exchanges of opinion, even when some of these described in official language are really excuses for what might in reality be drunken orgies. Modern marxist officialese works through consensus, avoidance of disagreement, dissent or offence. Blandness is its trademark. We believe that Várady has caught the essence of its style, both in feeling and language. He says in his own words: 'I tried to describe patterns of thinking and rhetoric schemes which are more and more independent of their origin, and which compose a world of their own, replacing horizons with a panorama of commonplaces. I had a feeling that these rhetoric patterns tend to be universal. The newly elected chairman of the fisherman's association of my home town, or the new president of some parliament, club, world trade association, national bar association, or any new chairman, is bound to deliver his inaugural address along the lines of the same melody. I was trying to identify these tunes in the context of a novel.' Might we point out that these 'melodies' have their western counterparts.

NWW is now published jointly by its original British publishers and Riverrun Press in the USA and remains one of the few continuing vehicles for shorter work by established writers that would otherwise be quickly lost in periodicals, and new work from both the English-speaking world and other cultures, often introducing world-class writers to the language for the first time. Published simultaneously in hard cover and paperback, it is especially interested to receive direct subscriptions for future issues and to receive the names and addresses of its supporters.

The Publishers

I
SYMMETRY

Harry Mulisch

Translated by Adrienne Dixon

Photograph of Harry Mulisch by Jaap Pieper

Born in Haarlem in 1927, of a father from Gablonz (at one time part of the Austro-Hungarian Empire) and a mother from Antwerp (but also of German-Austrian descent), Harry Mulisch grew up in an international family circle where the first books he read were from his father's solely foreign collection. Although he is best known as a prolific novelist, short story writer and poet, he is also a playwright and has written a number of non-fiction works including a study of Wilhelm Reich, a treatise on spelling reforms in Dutch and an eye-witness account of life in post-revolution Cuba. He is currently engaged on an ambitious project to be called nothing less than *The Composition of the World*. In 1977 he was awarded the Dutch State Prize for Literature and the Constantijn Huygens award. *The Boundary* (NWW 17), one of his most recent stories, has been made into a short film and the film of his novel *Two Women* (published earlier this year by John Calder) was premièred at the 1979 Cannes film festival in an English language version. *Symmetry* was published in a collection entitled *Old Air* of which the title story will appear in NWW 19.

SYMMETRY

I

It cannot be ruled out that one day in the winter of 1871 (while the Commune was being proclaimed in Paris) a blizzard may have been chasing past the statues of the saints on the Charles Bridge in Prague. Below, the Vltava carries its ice floes, while above the moon and the stars, and, invisible behind grey clouds, the ancient alchemists' and as yet far from Communist city lies around, gnarled and twisted like the roots of a tree. And it is as if I now see my grandfather before me, a nineteen year old student in his back room in the inner city, at the foot of Hradčany Hill.

The tall, tiled stove is hot and he is standing in front of the mirror, putting on his black tie. He looks into a pale, smooth-shaven face with thin lips and slightly slanting eyes, his brown hair is long and sleek. Behind him, a table with books and papers; Menger's *Grundsätze der Volkswirtschafts-lehre*, just published, lies open. (Marx' *Kapital*, the first part of which has come out a few years earlier, is nowhere to be seen.) He buttons up his waistcoat and fastens his silver watch chain to the top button. He would prefer to stay at home in this weather but considers it wasteful not to use his ticket. (In later years he will be a bank manager.)

There has been a notice in the hall of Charles University announcing the lecture:

Prof. Dr. Ernst Mach
will speak on
SYMMETRY
in the German Casino
8 o'clock

Friends claimed that Mach was a genius, not only in

physics but also in philosophy. He had become a professor seven years earlier, at the age of twenty six. My grandfather listens placidly to such talk by his jealous friends. He himself has no ambitions of that kind; all he desires are a good position, a pleasant house, a loving wife and three obedient children. Still, he wouldn't mind seeing a genius in action just for once, for he has never yet seen such a person in the flesh.

Bending forward, one hand in the pocket of his coat, the other holding his hat down on his head, my grandfather makes his way across the Charles Bridge to the German Casino. A vicious cold, different from that between the houses, comes at him from the river. Can I say that one quarter of me is already slumbering deep beneath that black overcoat, the front and shoulders of which are rapidly becoming white? Of course I can say that, who is to stop me – although the murderers would have it that a man cannot be quartered until after the event. Under his boots crunches the snow which transforms the light of gaslamps into a dreamy glow. The black statues too have become white on one side. Far below, he hears the ice floes knocking against the piers. There he goes, lonely, between one bank and the other, caught within the nineteenth century, his nose red with cold.

Passing through a low gateway he arrives at a trapezium-shaped square. Here the snow suddenly falls softly; in front of the Casino lies a large pool of yellow light. People emerge from the approach roads on foot and in carriages, in a woolly silence, the horses with bursts of steam coming from their nostrils, as if they do not want to lag behind the machines that are shortly to oust them from the world. Top hats, walking sticks, beribboned skirts. He hardly looks about him, yet it is the sort of scene which, years later, will suddenly appear in his memory – on his deathbed perhaps; the illumined building and the people in the silent snow, seeming to say how good life was, how it will never be again. Perhaps he will then wonder when that could have been, that winter evening; but Mach's lecture will have vanished from his memory. (In 1915 he will die; in retrospect it seems as if it was all rather pointless: his good position, the pleasant house, the loving wife and the three obedient children, – because it is not now.)

Symmetry is not a subject over which my grandfather normally torments his brain. It forms no part of his studies, unless it were the symmetry between assets and liabilities, on the left and right hand sides of the balance sheet, but then that is more a question for the bookkeepers. In contrast to Paris, (where the people are now arming themselves) symmetry does not occur at all in Prague, where everything is asymmetrical, crooked, like the Charles Bridge, curving, slanting, tortuous. Here it is not Descartes who reigns, with his spirit in the machine, but Rabbi Löw, who made the Golem. And perhaps this is precisely why it becomes so crowded in the overheated lecture room. People are eager to learn about this outlandish phenomenon, symmetry, in the same way as they like hearing about conditions on the moon.

II

The popularized scientific lecture, held in Prague that evening by the young professor, was later published so that we know that he did in fact start off with an observation about the moon.

'An ancient philosopher,' so he began, having silenced the applause of welcome with an almost ruthless gesture, 'once said that people who racked their brains about the conditions on the moon reminded him of people who discussed the government and the political institutions of a country they knew only by name. The true philosopher must direct his gaze inward, he should examine himself and his moral views; nothing else would ever lead anywhere. If this philosopher were to rise from the dead and reappear among us, ladies and gentlemen, he would be astounded to see how totally different things are today.'

The speaker had straight, back-combed hair and a large beard – not as large, it is true, as the beards of professors older than himself, of whom there were some in the audience, but still large enough for his mouth to be invisible behind the hair as he spoke. Above the moustaches stood the right-angled triangle of a narrow pointed nose, steel-rimmed spectacles straddling the tip of the hypothenuse. So this was what a genius looked like. Apart from the lectern and the easel and blackboard there stood also on the platform a tripod supporting a large mirror which was obviously going to be used for demonstrations later on. The grand piano had presumably been left there from last night; a concert perhaps, a Liszt recital, or a wedding party. Pulling the cuff out of one sleeve of his long coat, Professor Mach went on to say that we knew more about the moon than about ourselves. The *mécanique céleste* had been drawn up, but a *mécanique sociale* or a *mécanique morale* still had to be written:

'Man has returned a little wiser from the space travels he was advised not to undertake. Having become acquainted with simple astronomical relations, he is now beginning to appraise his small distorted Self with a critical eye. It sounds absurd and yet it is true: after having devoted ourselves to the moon we can now start with psychology.' As a small example of this he would now talk about the fact that some things are pleasing to us while others are not.

My grandfather crossed his legs and settled down to listen. From time to time he cast a furtive glance at the mirror on the platform in which he could see the pretty face of a girl in the front row. Tucked into the side of her pinned-up hair was a red flower; she gazed up admiringly at the thirty-three year old genius, and something like jealousy began to stir in my grandfather.

Repetition. Symmetry. Mach pointed to the mirror and observed that in it a right hand becomes a left hand, a right ear a left ear, but that on our body a left hand can never replace a right hand or a left ear a right ear, despite all similarity of form. The mirror image of an object can never take the place of that object. A watch in a mirror is no longer a watch. At this remark he raised a forefinger and interwove a pregnant silence during which my grandfather had the strange sensation of time running backward into the past. It made him miss the next few sentences but he picked up the thread again when the professor remarked that our body, like a Gothic cathedral, is vertically symmetrical: the imaginary mirror intersects us vertically. On the other hand, a lakeside landscape and its reflection are horizontally symmetrical. Why was it that vertical symmetries are immediately obvious to us, whilst horizontal ones are rarely noticed? Having thrown a questioning look around the room he stepped away from the lectern and wrote four letters on the blackboard:

d   b
q   p

Young children, he said, frequently confuse d and b, as well and p and q, but never d and q or b and p. At these words a murmur of agreement rippled through the audience, coming from mothers and schoolteachers. He smiled and said this was because the pairs d – b and q – p are vertically symmetrical and seem to the child to belong together, whereas it perceives no connection between the horizontally symmetrical pairs d – q and b – p.

My grandfather noticed that at this point several members of the audience were groping in their pockets for paper to take notes, meanwhile licking the tips of their pencils. Mach saw it too, and to allow them a little more time he gave another example: two porcelain statuettes, each representing a girl with a red flower in her hair, one on the left, the other on the right, can easily be interchanged, but a face turned upside down is unrecognizable, we know that from the nursery too! My grandfather saw her blushing in the mirror and his jealousy of the speaker's power grew.

Well now, what was the cause of all this? The cause of all this was that our eyes themselves also form a vertically symmetrical system. They are not identical. If they are interchanged – by means of a simple prismatic device – we enter at once into a totally new world. He stooped and took an odd-looking pair of wooden spectacles out of a case that stood by the side of the lectern. 'In these,' he said, holding the contraption aloft, 'all that is concave is convex, all that is convex is concave; all that is near is far and all that is far is near. Anyone who is interested can take a look presently.'

At this moment, the student sitting in front of my grandfather leaned aside and whispered to his neighbour: 'They should invent such a thing for time.'

'What do you mean?'

'In which the most distant past comes closest. That would be something!'

'Ssh,' said my grandfather.

Professor Mach spoke very clearly and slowly. Whenever

he uttered a slightly more difficult statement – for instance, that a straight line can be both horizontally and vertically symmetrical with itself – he paused and let his eyes rove over the audience with a roguish sidelong glance, like a conjuror who has yet again pulled the ace of diamonds from under his collar. Occasionally he said very quickly something which nobody understood, like: 'The reason why one can immediately visualize the first and second differentials of a curve but not the higher ones, is of course that the first indicates the gradient of the tangent and therefore the deviation from the line of symmetry, and the second the curvature and therefore the rate of change of gradient.' At such statements he invariably looked towards a particular point in the audience, where my grandfather then saw a balding pate nodding in agreement.

Suddenly he called out: 'Consider a piano in a mirror!'

He called it out loudly, like a command, so that here and there heads that had dozed off shot up. (Perhaps this was the moment at which, far away in Simbirks, little Vladimir Ilyich, not yet a year old, began to cry because he had lost the teddybear he always took to bed with him; later he would write that Mach's philosophy was to natural science as Judas' kiss was to Jesus Christ.) He stepped away from the lectern again and wheeled the tripod with mirror to the other side of the grand piano, so that the girl suddenly vanished from it and the keyboard appeared.

A piano like that one, he said, pointing at the mirror, had never been made. The low notes were on the right, the high ones on the left. If one were to play a melody in minor, one would hear a melody in major, and vice versa. Many of those present had probably at one time or another watched a pianist giving a concert in a hall of mirrors – but had anyone ever wondered what the pianist in the mirror was actually playing? He looked inquiringly around the audience. After all, sound was not reflected by mirrors, it was merely re-echoed by them, and conversely, the music played by the mirror pianist remained hidden within the mirror. (This remark did not form part of the text of his lecture, it was extempore.) It was obviously out of the question that such a costly mirror piano should ever be built, nor was this necessary, as it was possible to experiment in a different way.

'I shall now play something,' said Mach, 'while looking in the mirror, and then I shall play back on this piano what I have seen.'

He looked in the mirror and played several bars of *Für Elise*, and then he replayed what he had observed. Great hilarity among the audience; it was indeed most, most extraordinary!

'*Von Elise!*' the student in front of my grandfather called out, and the laughter increased, as people turned to their neighbours and laughingly repeated the remark.

Mach stroked his beard; he too was laughing. The joke seemed to please him. There appeared something defenceless in the positivist's intelligent, untragic face. Then he took the score of *Für Elise* from the piano and showed it to the audience, which resulted in more laughter. But this was only because they were all laughing already; there was nothing funny in it per se, and it was, in fact, the beginning of a new experiment. It turned out that lying flat on top of the piano there was a second mirror, above which he now positioned the score.

'And now,' he said, having once again admonished his listeners to silence with the same ruthless gesture as before, 'I shall play the notes I see in the mirror.'

Straightening his back he played the mirrored notes, and the same futuristic music which the mirror-Mach had played were heard again. Yes indeed, it was all most, most remarkable.

III

My grandfather has uncrossed his legs and listens spellbound. But although the professor has not yet completed his extraordinary demonstrations, I now take my leave of him and of the gentleman with the balding skull and of the student who for all I know may be a genius too, and of the girl with the red flower in her pinned-up hair (who will perhaps one day become my grandmother, in which case my grandfather will remember this evening forever). We shall never see them again. All this must remain unfinished – even though it has long since been finished and forgotten – and I leave them behind, in that German Casino, far away in 1871.

On the last but one occasion that I was myself in Prague, on Friday 27 December 1968 (when my father, in his turn, had also died) I had only a few hours to spare. I was passing through on my way to Cuba – the legitimate heiress of the Paris Commune – and between planes I took a stroll around the city. It was gloomy and cold. The days between Christmas and the New Year are a no-man's land with which nobody quite knows what to do. Through a grey mist in which hurried figures scurried through the dark, twisting streets, large snow flakes fell on the disconsolate Christmas trees still standing spaced out along the pavements. From public buildings red stars with gold hammers and sickles radiated a tremendous power. In my lightweight summer clothes, suitable for the tropics from where I would not return before spring, protected only by my Dutch umbrella, I walked across the Charles Bridge. From time to time, Czechs in long overcoats and big fur hats cast glances at me which made it quite clear that they had given up trying to understand everything in life. At home in Amsterdam I had followed, these last few days, the voyage of Apollo 8, in which the first men had left the earth's pull in order to circle the moon. I looked at my watch and saw to my surprise that in exactly three minutes the capsule would return to the earth's atmosphere, above the Pacific Ocean. I decided to experience this moment on the bridge.

By the statue of St Nepomuk who was thrown into the water at this point and now sported a hat of snow, I stood still and waited. I shivered with cold, I might as well have been naked, and yet I was sure I would not fall ill. Far down, the big flakes suddenly became part of the Vltava so that it seemed as if they had never existed. All around, the city with its spires and, higher up, the motionless hill with the walled cathedral, lay silent under the clouds, on the earth. When the three minutes had expired I walked on, – knowing that on the other side of the planet, somewhere in the summer over the blue ocean, the capsule had now plunged into the atmosphere like the head of a match strikes the side of a box, at a speed of Mach 33.

II
THE LAKE

A.R. Lamb

Photograph of A.R. Lamb

A.R. Lamb was born in 1949 and has worked mostly at manual jobs. The story included in this volume is taken from an unpublished collection of which *The Glazed Eye* appeared in NWW 13.

THE LAKE

Wilf looked up to see a woman standing in front of him. He looked down again immediately and tried to make out that he was profoundly involved in choosing which sandwich he should eat next.

'You'd better get up,' said the woman.

'You what?' said Wilf.

'You'd better get up.'

'Why?'

'Rosa is floating in the middle of the lake.'

'So what?'

'She can only float. She can't swim. She can't stay in the water much longer. She'll have to be picked up soon. She'll have to be picked up very soon. She might already be dead.'

'How did she get out there in the first place?'

'I supppose she just drifted out without knowing it. She always keeps her eyes closed. The big danger is if she goes to sleep. If she goes to sleep she'll drown.'

'I've never heard of anyone who can float and not swim,' he remarked.

'I expect there's a lot of things you haven't heard of,' she replied.

Should I believe her? he thought. I don't know. She might be telling the truth. If she's telling the truth you ought to believe her.

He looked at his watch:

'I've got to be back at work in ten minutes,' he announced.

'I'll pay you for the time you miss,' she said, pulling some notes out of her pocket and showing them to him.

'What if I get the sack?'

'I shouldn't think you'll get the sack for saving

someone's life. But if you do I'm sure Rosa would give you a job.'

'Has she got a lot of money?'

'She's rolling in it.'

Wilf got up and walked down to the lake.

'There she is,' said the woman, pointing.

He did indeed see something floating out in the middle. It was impossible to tell whether it was a body or not.

'You can take the boat. It's hers. Here's some money.'

'Aren't you going, then?' exclaimed Wilf, as he took the money. 'I mightn't be able to get her into the boat on my own.'

'No. I don't think I'll bother. I've probably got better things to do.'

She was already backing away from him as she spoke. Now she turned and climbed quickly out of his sight.

What do you make of her, then? thought Wilf. Must be off her head. So you think she's made it up now? No, because there is something floating out there. But it might be a mine which'll go off as soon as I get near it. And it might be a woman. And it might be a mine pretending to be a woman. All you can say about that object is that it's longer than it's wide and lighter than water. Just think for a minute about all the objects in that class. I don't want to. The only object I'm interested in is that one out there. It isn't a possibility, it's a certainty, and the only way you can find out which certainty it is is by going and having a look. That's rubbish. Even supposing it's a living woman at this moment, when I get there it might be a corpse. Oh, bugger it. You'll have to go now.

He went along to the boat. It contained, besides a pair of oars, some clothes and a towel. That's pretty good evidence for it being a woman, he thought. He took off his boots and socks; rolled up his trousers; dragged the boat into the water; climbed aboard; put his boots and socks back on; put the oars through the rowlocks; began to row.

As he drew near he saw that the object was really a woman. She was wearing a black wet-suit. An aura of faint colours seemed to hover above her. She was moving her arms and legs slightly to keep herself horizontal. Her eyes were closed.

'Hello,' said Wilf.

She didn't reply. He rowed a bit nearer.

'Hello?'

She opened her eyes and smiled up at him. The aura shrank and vanished.

'I've come to rescue you,' he said.

She looked towards the shore.

'I'm right out in the middle,' she remarked.

'You ought to watch what you're doing.'

'I can't swim and I can't keep my eyes open.'

'So I've been told,' he said. 'Do you want rescuing or not?'

'Yes, please.'

He just managed to get her into the boat without capsizing it. She sat in the stern facing him and began to dry her hair with the towel.

'Thankyou,' she said.

He began to row back towards the shore.

'Wait a minute,' she said. 'Where are you going?'

'Going back. Where do you think I'm going?'

'You're going the wrong way. I want to be the other side.'

'I'm sorry,' said Wilf, carrying on rowing. 'I've wasted enough time as it is. I've got to get back to work.'

'Please turn round,' she said, with apparent anxiety. 'If we go any nearer to that side I've had it.'

'Why?'

'Miriam will shoot me.'

Wilf stopped rowing.

'Who's Miriam and why will she shoot you?' he enquired, in a patronising voice.

'She's a sniper, and she'll shoot me because she wants me dead.'

'A sniper!' laughed Wilf. 'How can anybody be a sniper?'

'It's easy. You just get yourself a gun, and some ammunition, and you go up in a tree and you snipe. There are probably masses of them about.'

She waved her arms as though to demonstrate that they might be all around the lake. Wilf grinned:

'How come I've never seen one, then?'

'You don't see snipers,' she said. 'By definition a sniper is invisible.'

Wilf stared at her. Why is she telling me this tommyrot? he thought. Whoever heard of snipers in trees round here? There's a lot of things you haven't heard of. You can't really believe it, can you? I can believe anything I like.

'But you must have already been across that side today for your boat to have been there,' he said.

'My boat?'' she queried. ''This isn't my boat.'

'Whose boat is it, then?'

'How the hell should I know? I thought it was yours.'

'And I suppose that towel isn't yours, and those clothes aren't yours.'

'No!' she exclaimed. 'How could they be?'

She seemed astonished by his questions. He felt sure that her astonishment was feigned.

'Is your name Rosa?' he asked.

'Yes,' she replied, frowning. 'How did you know that?'

'The woman who asked me to rescue you –'

'What woman?' she interrupted. 'You were asked to do it?'

'Yes. I thought she was your friend. She even paid me to do it.'

Rosa let out a short, anguished scream.

'That woman!' she exclaimed. 'What'll she think of next?'

She leaned across; gripped his forearms tightly; delved into his eyes:

'Don't you see? That was Miriam who paid you. It's a trap. She's banking on you not believing me. She's banking on you rowing me to within range of her gun. She's set it all up. She's up there in one of those trees.'

'This is ridiculous,' said Wilf. 'If she wanted to kill you then why didn't she just get in the boat herself and row out and shoot you. It may as well have been her in the boat for all you'd have known about it.'

'Simple,' said Rosa, quietly. 'She's terrified of water ... she can hardly even bear to go near it.'

On an impulse, Wilf turned the boat around and began rowing towards the other shore.

'Oh, thankyou. Thankyou so much,' said Rosa.

She smiled:

'I'd give anything to be able to see her face right now.

She'll be cursing; she'll be raging. With a bit of luck she might even fall out of her tree ... It was a pretty stupid idea though, wasn't it?'

'There's no need to carry on with this rubbish,' said Wilf. 'You're not getting your own way because I believe you but because I just want to save time and trouble.'

'You're wonderful,' she declared.

Wilf scowled. He listened to the rhythmic tapping of the small waves against the bow, and enjoyed the sensation of speed caused by rowing into the wind.

'See that white house over there in amongst the trees,' she said.

He turned round and saw.

'Could you make for it. There's a landing-jetty just in front of it.'

'Is that where you live?'

She nodded.

There was a man sitting on the end of the jetty, dangling his bare feet in the water. He helped to pull the boat in.

'I was just about to come and get you when I saw you were already being rescued,' he said, addressing Rosa.

'That's alright, Tom,' she said. 'Thankyou. What time are you leaving?'

'Five o'clock.'

She got out of the boat.

'Will you come into the house?' she said to Wilf.

He shook his head:

'No. I must be getting back to work. With a bit of luck I won't have been missed.'

She and Tom exchanged glances.

'I don't want to alarm you unduly,' she said to Wilf. 'But I wouldn't be surprised if Miriam's attitude towards you wasn't completely friendly. You've spoiled her silly little plan. I doubt if she'll kill you, but she may well take a pot-shot at an arm or a leg.'

'Oh yes?' said Wilf, grinning.

'Yes ... What do you think, Tom?'

She told Tom the details of the plot as she saw it. When she'd finished Tom shook his head slowly:

'She'll be mad, that's for sure. I wouldn't risk it if I were you, mate.'

Wilf looked from one to the other of them. They're not
joking, he thought. Of course they are. They're up to
something. She's trying to trap you. She's trying to make a
fool of you. But what if it's just as she says it is. Then there's
a good chance of you getting shot when you row back. No.
It's impossible. It doesn't make sense. I'm going to go.
There's no-one there to shoot me.

He pushed against the jetty. The boat moved out. He set
the oars.

'Goodbye,' he said, breezily.

'Goodbye and thankyou,' said Rosa. 'Don't worry too
much. She'll probably be so angry that she won't be able to
shoot straight.'

Great, thought Wilf. If she aims for my arm she'll hit my
heart.

He rowed back across the lake as powerfully as he could,
the effort of his muscles testifying to a world in which he
was both alone and invincible.

The bullet tore through the flesh on his left forearm.

His first impulse was to throw himself flat on the bottom
of the boat. His second impulse was to get out of the boat
and try to swim under water. His third impulse, the one he
obeyed, was to turn the boat about and row like a dingbat
towards where he had just come from. Even when he knew
he was well out of range, and even though the blood was
pouring from his wound, he didn't let up, couldn't let up.

He climbed out at the jetty and strode up to the house,
holding his arm tightly above the elbow. He kicked on the
door a few times, accompanying his kicks with curses. Rosa
opened the door. She was dressed.

'I could have been bloody dead,' he said, accusingly.

'I'm sorry,' she replied.

She led him along to a bathroom. She washed and
bandaged his arm.

'You'll be alright,' she declared. 'You won't lose any
more blood. It'll heal up in no time at all.'

'I'd like to sit down,' said Wilf.

She took him into a sitting-room. He sat down in an
armchair. He wasn't angry any more. He'd been shot; he'd
lost a fair amount of blood: the combination of these two
factors had turned his mind into a frivolous place where

cause and effect wore the same clothes and danced the
same dance, where the heaviest questions fluttered about
like leaves.

He tried to work out how he was going to get home safely.
He suspected that at some point along whichever path he
chose to take, Miriam was already looking through her
sights at him; that her finger was already pulling back the
trigger; that the bullet was already emerging from the
barrel; that his heart was already being punctured. And he
realised that even if he avoided this fate, and a helicopter
dropped him at his door, then Miriam was already in his
room with a smile on her face and a neat revolver in her
hand. Although he was quite able to believe that they
referred to some sort of truth, these imaginings didn't
depress him. He'd been shot and he'd escaped with the
mildest of wounds: this was enough to make him feel as
invulnerable as a corpse.

'Why don't you get the police onto her?' he asked.

He saw that he'd been thinking of Miriam as though
there was nothing outside her, as though she wasn't
bounded by society. He saw that the bullet which now lay
on the bottom of the lake had offended against the law, as
well as against his body.

'How can I?' said Rosa, sitting down. 'They wouldn't
believe me. And if they did believe me they wouldn't be able
to find her.'

'They'd find her,' asserted Wilf. 'They're not stupid.
And if we both went along, and I showed them my wound,
they'd certainly believe you.'

She smiled and shook her head:

'But even supposing they found her, and even supposing
they found the gun, and even supposing they proved that
she'd fired the gun at you, what would be the result? She'd
be put in prison for a couple of years, that's all. It wouldn't
stop her wanting to kill me: it wouldn't prevent her from
carrying on trying to kill me when she got out, would it?'

'I don't know. She might realise that her way of going
about things is unacceptable, that when she offends against
the law she offends against herself.'

Rosa laughed. Wilf laughed too, understanding that
there might be something inherently idiotic in what he'd
said.

'What does she want to kill you for anyway?' he asked, offhandedly, as though this was the least important aspect of the matter.

'It's a long story.'

'Oh, I see,' said Wilf, curtailing the subject.

He wasn't particularly interested. His mind had descended from frivolity to its more usual, ponderous state. He was asking himself sensible questions like: Am I still in danger? Have I lost my job? If I haven't lost it, do I dare go back to it tomorrow?

Tom came in, placed a tray on the table in front of them, proceeded to pour three cups of tea.

'How do you feel?' he asked, handing Wilf a cup.

'Not so bad,' said Wilf. 'More relieved than anything.'

Tom nodded. Then he went out of the room, returning after a few seconds with a suitcase. He put the case down on the carpet and opened it. There were some clothes on the top. He took the clothes out, to reveal a mass of banknotes. Wilf looked away almost immediately, feeling as though he had seen something which he oughtn't to have seen. If he had ever had such an enormous amount of money himself he would certainly not have displayed it in front of a stranger.

'Have you got enough?' said Rosa.

'I don't know,' replied Tom. 'I'm just going to count it roughly and see.'

He poured the money out, and then began putting it back in wads, counting each note. He'd only done about a tenth of the total when he said:

'Oh, I can't be bothered.'

He threw the rest of the money and his clothes back into the suitcase and shut it.

'There's loads there,' he commented.

Rosa turned to Wilf and said:

'Tom's leaving me today. How would you like his job?'

'What is your job?' said Wilf to Tom.

'It's dead easy,' replied Tom. 'It's just a matter of going out to pick Rosa up when she floats too far. That's about all there is to it.'

'Why are you leaving?' asked Wilf.

'I want to go round the world.'

Wilf guffawed, perhaps taking this statement to mean

something different from what it did mean. Then he turned
to Rosa:

'How much would I get paid?'

She shrugged, as if to indicate that this was a question of
no importance:

'You can start off with twice as much as you're getting in
your present job, and you can live in the house for free.'

Wilf couldn't help showing the immediate pleasure he
felt at this astounding offer.

'And that's really all I'd have to do? It seems a lot for a
little.'

'It's a very responsible job,' she said. 'And it's a job
which has got to be done, or else I wouldn't survive.'

Tom stood up.

'I may as well go now and get a head start,' he said.
'You don't need me any more, do you?'

'No, that's alright,' said Rosa.

Tom picked up his case. Rosa stood up. They both
looked down at Wilf.

'Think about it,' said Rosa.

'Goodbye,' said Tom.

Wilf nodded. They went out of the room, and out of
earshot.

What do you make of that, then? he thought. I don't
know. It seems too good to be true. It's so good it must be
bad. It's probably a trap. She's probably going to kill me
when I'm asleep and dissect my body. Why would she want
to do that? She's a psychopath and an amateur biologist.

He laughed at his own joke. Then he went on to suspect
that Miriam was in league with Rosa, and that the whole
train of events which had trundled by since Miriam had
interrupted his lunch had been engineered with the aim of
getting him to accept this job, with the aim of murdering
him in his sleep.

This is a lot of rubbish, he thought. Nobody's going to
murder you. If you stay here you'll be as safe as houses.

He provisionally awarded the palm to this last statement.
And anyway, he could always lock his door at night. He
could always make sure that he ate the same food as she
ate. The idea of cutting himself off from his immediate past
appealed to him strongly. To never go back to his job. To
never go back to his lodgings. He felt he ought to bow to

such powerful concepts.

Rosa came back into the room.
　'He's gone,' she declared, sitting down.
　She looked a few tears older.
　'Have you decided?' she asked. 'You don't have to stay
a minute longer than you want to – as long as you don't
leave when I'm on the lake.'
　'Yes. Alright. I'll take the job. Why not?'
　As soon as he'd said this, and realised that he was now her
servant, his attitude towards her changed. He felt that he
had sunk somewhat below her. He felt that she had
automatically confiscated his liberty, so that he was no
longer free to ask the questions which he might have
wanted to ask now that his own worries were negated.
　"I'll show you round," she said, standing up.
　He followed her into various rooms. One of the rooms
upstairs she described as having belonged to Tom, and as
now belonging to him. He lingered there for a while,
concluding that the room was a lot more attractive than the
one in which he had spent the night before.
　They went outside by way of the back door. There was a
patch of cultivated garden surrounded by rhododendron.
Beyond the rhododendron stood the same assortment of
trees as could be found anywhere around the lake. He
followed her through the trees until they came to a tall
wooden fence. A large white dog stepped silently out of the
undergrowth of nettles and ferns and stood facing them,
motionless except for the twitching of its nose. The dog
appeared to be staring at Rosa. Rosa appeared to be
staring at the dog. After a couple of minutes of this Wilf
began to feel uncomfortable, began to imagine that there
was some kind of bizarre communion going on.
　'Is he yours?' he asked.
　'He's mine as much as you are mine,' she replied,
gradually transporting her gaze from the dog to Wilf.
　What's that supposed to mean? he thought.
　'What's his name?' he said.
　'I don't know what his real name is. At the moment I
think of him as Walter. The only time you'll hear him bark
is if Miriam gets within rifle range of this property. By the
way, what do they call you?'

'Wilf.'

The dog slid past them. They carried on along the fence, until they came to a gate. Then they walked back on the drive which snaked around to the front of the house.

'The fence virtually touches the water at both ends,' she remarked. 'The gate can only be opened by those who I want to open it.'

'Sounds pretty secure.'

'Yes. I'm not worried. As long as you do your job properly I can expect to carry on living.'

When they got back to the house Rosa announced that she was going to her room; that he was to feel free to wander wherever he pleased; that dinner would be at seven o'clock.

Wilf went outside again; went down to the jetty. The boat had drifted some of the way back across the lake. It was a little lower in the water than it ought to have been, perhaps weighed down by the bullet-hole in its stern. The surface of the lake was calm. There was even a slight haze. He stayed there for a long time, imagining that he had become as involuntary as the boat, as thoughtless as the water, as vague as the haze.

He returned to the house and sat down at the dinner table with Rosa. They helped themselves from the same dishes, so he felt fairly sure he wasn't being poisoned. He couldn't restrain himself from devouring an enormous amount of food. Rosa ate very little.

'How's your arm?' she enquired, when the meal was over.

'Alright.'

'Is it well enough to do a bit of rowing later on?'

He shrugged his shoulders, then pulled hard with his left hand against the seat of his chair. This action caused only a slight pain.

'I should think so.'

'I shall be going into the water in a few minutes.'

She got up and left the room. When she returned she was dressed in her wet-suit.

'You'd better come down with me,' she said.

He followed her until they came to a rowing-boat hauled up some twenty yards from the jetty.

'This is your boat,' she said. 'There's a torch under the seat there.'

They walked a little way along towards the jetty.

'As far as I can tell it will take me just over three hours before I get within range, so if you pick me up in three hours from now there shouldn't be any problems. If the wind gets up you'll have to set out that much sooner.'

'Does the wind always blow from this side?' he asked.

'Of course it does,' she snapped.

'How much time should I allow for finding you?' he asked, as she walked into the water.

'As long as you like,' she said, sarcastically. 'Just don't disturb me before it's necessary.'

When the water was up to her waist she turned around, lay down on her back, and closed her eyes.

Wilf watched her go. He didn't know what she was up to and he couldn't be bothered to imagine. At this particular moment he was more interested in himself. The silence and the twilight had combined to make him doubt the strength of his existence. He felt as though he might evaporate at any moment.

If I evaporate what'll happen to the world? he thought. If you evaporate the world will collapse. Really? That means I must be holding the world up. And if I'm holding the world up I must be stronger than the world. And if I'm stronger than the world I can't possibly evaporate.

This argument proved valid: instead of evaporating he turned and walked back up to the house.

As he got into the hall he was surprised to hear someone singing softly in the living-room. The voice was female. The melody was sweet. Wilf crept back outside and peered in through the window. The owner of the voice was sitting on the settee. It wasn't Miriam. He went back in. The melody resolved itself as he turned the door-handle and entered the room. The woman looked round at him and smiled.

'How are you?' she said.

Wilf nodded.

'Don't worry,' she said. 'I'm a friend of Rosa's.'

'Afraid she isn't in,' said Wilf.

'Of course she isn't,' said the woman, laughing.

She held out her hand:

'Come and sit down,' she said.

Why not? thought Wilf. He felt attracted towards her. He went further into the room. The woman introduced herself as Magda. He sat down in an armchair.

'What have you done to your arm?' she enquired.

'Oh, a bullet wound,' he replied, not without a tinge of smugness.

'An accident?'

'No. Deliberate. Someone took a shot at me this afternoon. A woman called Miriam. Do you know her?'

'Yes. I know her.'

'If you know her then perhaps you can tell me why she hates Rosa and wants to kill her.'

'Of course I can tell you. She's jealous of her. By killing her she can inherit Rosa's love of water and so be able to float on the lake herself.'

'I see,' said Wilf.

'When Rosa dies tonight Miriam will immediately become capable of floating on the lake in the same way as Rosa has done, and will be able to set about achieving the same ends.'

'What do you mean, when Rosa dies tonight?' he said, astonished. 'You make it sound as though it's a certainty.'

'It is,' she declared. 'Rosa will be shot tonight.'

'Do you want a bet?' said Wilf.

'She'll float into range in less than three hours time. Miriam's bullet will pierce her heart.'

'It won't, because I'll pick her up before she gets into range. That's my job. That's what I'm here for.'

She grinned:

'You think that's what you're here for, but unfortunately the reality of why you're here has nothing to do with your idea of why you're here.'

'I'm not worried. Nothing can stop me rowing out and rescuing her.'

'What if your arms were broken? It's impossible to row with broken arms.'

It occurred to Wilf that she wasn't joking; that they weren't alone in the house; that there were two strong men waiting outside the door; that they would enter the room at her command and break his arms.

'In fact it would probably be a very good idea for me to

break your arms,' she said, casually. 'If your arms were broken you'd have the perfect explanation to give to anyone who might ask you why you didn't rescue Rosa, why you didn't do your job. You couldn't be blamed. You'd feel no guilt. You wouldn't even need to tell them that it was I who broke your arms – you could say that two strong men did it.'

Wilf nodded, as though agreeing with her. He wasn't bothered now. He felt that it was impossible for a woman to break his arms.

'Yes,' he said. 'It's an excellent idea.'

Magda suddenly jumped up. Wilf saw to his amazement that she was holding an iron bar in her right hand. She raised the bar. There was no lack of conviction about the expression on her face. She began to bring the bar down upon him. Had he stayed where he was his left arm would have been smashed. But instead of staying where he was he leaped forward for all he was worth, leaving the chair to take the blow. By the time she had turned round he had grabbed the poker from the fireplace and installed himself behind the other armchair. But she merely smiled and lobbed her bar so that it landed on the seat of his chair, so that he could pick it up if he wanted to. Then she sat down in her previous position on the settee. Her apparent calmness made Wilf relax a little.

'Perhaps if you can understand the system it won't be necessary to break your arms,' she suggested.

Wilf shrugged:

'Go on.'

'It's simply that there are some events which are inevitable before they've taken place and other events which are only inevitable after they've taken place. Whether you have your arms broken or not is purely incidental to your failure to rescue Rosa. Broken arms won't cause you to fail. They'll merely be a decoration upon the fact of Rosa's death. Rosa's death is unalterable; the decorations upon it are not. The best thing for you to do, the least painful decoration, would be to go home right now and pretend that nothing had happened. After a while you wouldn't even have to pretend; you'd begin to believe it.'

Wilf sighed. If things were as she said they were; if he was a part of the system which she had described then perhaps it would be best for him just to go home.

Nobody'll ever know that I've been here, he thought. I won't be implicated in her murder. And it's not as if I'm running away from her or being disloyal. If there's nothing I can do to save her then I may as well be out of it. How can you think like that? The system doesn't work. The system doesn't exist. It's riddled with fallacies. She's just invented it in order to prevent you from doing your job and rescuing Rosa. She's hand in glove with Miriam, can't you see that? It might appear to be riddled with fallacies, but it would appear like that whether it existed or not. My thoughts are based upon another system, therefore I'm bound to think that this system is fallacious. I can't think about this system because the structure of my thought is different from the structure of the system.

The trouble was that even though he couldn't quite conceive of the system for the very reasons which he himself recognised he could sympathise with it; he could feel that it bore some relation to the truth; he could easily believe that free-will did not permeate the universe, and that parts of the future already existed. He was familiar with the system in an implicit way which made him attracted towards it when he heard it made explicit by someone else.

But that doesn't mean that things will be as she said they will be, he thought. If it is success and not failure which lies in the future then that doesn't even mean that the system is invalid. It might easily just mean that she is lying.

I'll get away from her, he decided. I'll go upstairs to my room. No, I'll go out on the lake right now and row around and wait until it's time to pick Rosa up.

'I'll go home, then,' he said, stepping out from behind the chair. 'I can see that there's no argument against what you've been saying.'

'That's good,' she said.

'Goodbye,' he said. 'I suppose I ought to say thankyou as well – you've saved me a lot of inconvenience.'

She went with him to the front door and even opened it for him.

'I'll go home along the road,' he informed her, as he stepped out into the darkness.

He made a show of going up the drive, grinding the gravel loudly with his feet. Then as soon as he was out of sight of the house he doubled back and ran down through the trees towards the lake.

He frantically dragged the boat into the water and clambered aboard. As he turned to feel for the oars the woman sat up and gazed at him calmly. Wilf groaned. For a while he was unable to speak. Then he said:

'Why are you trying to stop me, if Rosa's death is inevitable?'

She shrugged her shoulders slightly:

'I suppose it's because I like you ... There's an infinite number of things which could happen to you between now and the time when Rosa gets into range. Some of those things could be pretty nasty. I don't want anything nasty to happen to you.'

She spoke in a soft voice and even went so far as to briefly press her hand against his knee.

Don't let yourself be taken in, he thought. This is just a lot of eyewash. Throw her out of the boat. I can't throw her out. She might drown, and even if she's guilty she surely doesn't deserve to drown; and even if she deserves to drown I can't be the one to drown her, I can't act in the name of the law.

The surface of the lake was unruffled by the tiny breeze. The moon made spasmodic appearances between clouds. The boat was now some fifteen yards from the shore.

She can swim, he concluded. She wouldn't have risked coming on the boat with me if she couldn't swim, and anyway we're probably not even out of her depth yet.

He suddenly leaned forward, grabbed her beneath her armpits, then stood up and pulled her so that she was half over the side of the boat. But that was as far as his efforts took him, because the next second it was he and not she who was colliding with the water, it was he who was going under and coming up and gasping for breath.

When the shock had subsided and he'd got himself under control he tried to swim back to the boat, but she pushed him away with one of the oars.

'Swim back to the shore,' she shouted. 'You fool. Swim back to the shore.'

He watched helplessly while she set the oars, turned the boat to face out towards the middle, and began to row. He still tried to swim after her, but was far too hampered by his clothes and his boots. Then he had the impression of something white and silent gliding past him in the direction of the boat, travelling faster than the boat. For a moment he could make no sense of what his eyes told him; for a moment he thought that nature was being superseded; then he realised that it was the white dog.

The dog caught up with the boat and somehow managed to climb aboard. There was a shout and a splash, and the dog was standing alone in the boat. Wilf couldn't tell whether the dog had actually attacked the woman or whether she had left the boat voluntarily. It didn't really matter much. What mattered was that the dog was in the boat and the woman was in the water.

That's great, felt Wilf. Everything's alright. She must have been wrong. White dogs are always right.

He began to swim towards the boat with as good a breast-stroke as he could manage. The dog almost immediately jumped into the water and started to swim back: he passed Wilf without turning his head. Wilf was fortunately able to restrain himself from telling the dog that he was a good boy.

Wilf got into the boat; took off his boots and emptied them out; took off his clothes and bandage and wrung them out. His arm was beginning to throb. He picked up the torch and discovered that the wound had opened slightly and a little bit of dark, thick blood was oozing away. He tied the bandage back on as well as he could, then he looked round for the woman, thinking that if she was in trouble he might at least be able to help her to the shore. But even after rowing around the vicinity he could see no sign of her and he was forced to realise that she'd probably drowned.

He was naked and shivering. His watch had stopped. There was no doubt in his mind that he must get to Rosa at once. The time for debating what he ought to believe had passed. He must trust in his vision of the white dog as being the embodiment of goodness. He must retain that vision at all costs and dismiss the terrors which Magda had predicted. He pointed the boat towards the middle; shone his torch out to make sure that there were no obstacles in his way; then began to row.

He rowed to where he estimated she would have reached. He shone the torch around.

She's not here, he thought. She's been made invisible. No, she's already dead. She's been swept along by a freak current into the path of Miriam's bullet.

Then he spied a little blur of colour hovering above the surface, rowed towards it, and saw with a stupendous relief that it was her and that her arms and legs were moving.

'Rosa!' he said, urgently. 'Rosa! Hello!'

She didn't open her eyes so he poked her with an oar. As soon as he had touched her she began to groan, loudly and eerily and continuously as though she was in great pain. For a moment he thought that she had already been shot, but he could find no puncture in her wet-suit.

'Rosa! What is it?' he shouted. 'You've got to get out!'

The groaning went on. He leaned out of the back of the boat and tried to get her in but her co-operation was so entirely lacking that he was forced to choose between letting go of her and letting part of the lake into the boat: he let go of her. She went under and when she came up she spluttered for a while but her groaning had ceased. He kept on repeating her name until eventually her eyes opened. He managed to get her to look at him by shining the torch at his own face and at the boat as well as at her.

'Can you hear me?' he asked.

'My heart,' she said. 'I've had the most terrible pain … I thought I was going to die.' Her voice was slurred. 'It's still there, but's not so bad now.'

She stared at him for a while and frowned:

'Why have you got no shirt on, and why have you disturbed me before time. I'm not paying you to come out here and interrupt me. You've just about killed me as it is.'

'Listen, Rosa, I had to …'

He told her quickly what had happened, concluding with the words:

'… so please get into the boat and let's go.'

'There's nothing else I can do now, is there?' she said.

He helped her into the boat. She sat there stony-faced while he rowed.

I wish I hadn't bloody bothered, he was thinking. I'll probably get quadruple pneumonia and she can't even say thankyou.

They reached the jetty and disembarked in silence.

'I don't suppose you've got any men's clothes I could

borrow,' he said, when they went into the house.

'There should be some in your room,' she replied.

He followed her upstairs. She provided him with a large towel, and showed him an assortment of clothes.

He pointed at his bandage: the blood was showing through.

'Do you think you could put another one on for me.'

She went out and came back with a little bowl of hot water, some cotton wool, some bandage. She washed and re-bandaged his arm.

'Come to my room when you're ready,' was all she said.

Wilf scowled at her back as she went out.

Why does she make me feel as though I ought to feel guilty when I've done the only thing I could do? he thought. What am I doing here anyway? Yes, what are you doing here? You surely don't belong in such an idiotic set-up.

By the time he was dressed he felt warm and strong; ready to face up to her; ready to tell her, if necessary, that he would leave tomorrow.

He knocked on the door of her room and went in.

She had changed and was sitting on the end of the bed.

'Have some brandy,' she said.

He helped himself.

'Sit down,' she said, indicating a chair.

Having sat down, he found that the level of his head was below the level of her head. The confidence with which he had entered the room began to fade.

'Before I left I asked you not to disturb me before it was necessary. Do you remember?'

'Yes,' he agreed. 'But I thought it was necessary ... Wasn't it necessary?'

'It's only ever necessary to disturb me in order to prevent me from coming into range of Miriam's rifle. There can't be any exceptions to that rule. Your job is to pick me up as near as possible to the moment when I come into range.'

'But I was frozen,' he said. 'I don't see what else I could have done. I just didn't know what was going on.'

'I'm not paying you to know what's going on,' she said, harshly.

Wilf emptied his glass, hoping that the alcohol would give him the courage to break out of the bubble of subservience which had formed around him; give him the

courage to stand up and tell her what she could do with her
job. He was sure there was no justice in the way she was
treating him.

She smiled at him; he looked away immediately; she
said:

'Now I expect you're wanting to resign.'

'Yes,' he said, the blood rushing to his forehead. 'I've
never had much of a taste for oppression.'

She laughed:

'You can leave when you like. If you want a job where
you'll be praised for being inefficient then go and find one.'

Wilf stared at the carpet.

You'd be silly to go now, he thought. It needn't always be
as bad as this. You'll be able to be equal to her in the end.
Think of the money, anyway.

'I'll see what it's like tomorrow,' he said.

'Fine,' she replied.

He heard a noise from the corridor. He saw the door-
handle turn. Then the door swung open and Magda
staggered into the room. She faced them without appearing
to see them; gave a soft moan; closed her eyes; and
collapsed onto the floor. Wilf jumped up and hurried over
to her. Her face was as white and as lifeless as porcelain.
Her dress was embroidered with thin green threads of slime
and weed. He turned to Rosa:

'What shall we do?' he asked, urgently.

Rosa was staring at Magda. Her face expressed a
mixture of hatred and anger.

'I don't care what you do,' she said, without taking her
eyes off Magda. 'Just get her out of here.'

'Oh, bloody hell,' muttered Wilf, disgusted by this
callousness.

He picked Magda up as gently as he could and carried
her round into his room. He laid her down on the bed.
Rosa's door slammed shut. Magda's pulse was slow and
faint.

She needs warmth, he thought. Warm her up and she'll
come back to life.

He tore her dress off her. She had nothing else on. There
was no colour in her body: her skin was white; her hair was
black. He rubbed her vigorously with the towel until she
was dry then he tucked her in beneath the bedclothes and

continued to rub her with his hands from the outside.

He could see that Rosa's lack of concern was understandable. After all, if the white dog hadn't interfered and won the battle which Wilf had lost then Rosa would be dead by now and Magda would have been just as instrumental to her death as Miriam. So why shouldn't Rosa be angry? And why should she care whether Magda lived or died? As far as he knew Rosa wasn't trying to kill anyone, whereas Miriam and Magda, either independently or co-operatively, were trying to kill Rosa. On this evidence alone Rosa and the white dog were in the right. But he was beginning to wonder whether Miriam and Magda were justified in wishing Rosa dead. He wouldn't have cared if he never saw Rosa again, yet as he gazed at the unconscious Magda he realised that he didn't only want her to come back to life in order to avoid the embarrassment of being saddled with a corpse. He was sure that she wasn't as evil as he had at one time postulated her to be. He might even have got his symbolism mixed up: perhaps the white dog wasn't inevitably allied with justice.

Eventually a little tinge of colour drifted back into Magda's cheeks. Her pulse became quicker and stronger. She opened her eyes. She focused upon him. She smiled.

'How do you feel?' he enquired.

'Perfect,' she sighed.

'Why do you want Rosa dead?'

She smiled again.

'I don't want her dead,' she asserted. 'If I'd wanted her dead she'd be dead by now.'

'How come?'

'I could have broken your arms couldn't I? I could have chopped up the boat. I could have done any number of things to prevent you from rescuing her. But I didn't Everything was done with the sole purpose of making you pick Rosa up when you did. The more drama and danger you experienced the more likely you were to pick her up immediately. Everything went exactly as I wanted it to go. Even the dog performed the trick I wanted him to perform. His trick was part of my trick and my trick worked.'

Wilf shook his head:

'I don't know what you're on about.'

She was silent for a while, then she said:

'What do you think of the system here? Don't you think it's absurd that Rosa should love the water while Miriam is terrified of it; that Rosa should be master of the lake while Miriam sits shivering up a tree? Isn't it an absurd system?'.

Wilf shrugged:

'Seems alright to me. It's the way things are, so it must be alright.'

'Ah, you're caught up in it already. Can't you even see that it might be better if it was different?'

'I suppose it'd be better for Rosa if Miriam gave up trying to shoot her, and it'd be better for Miriam if she managed to kill Rosa.'

'But that's still part of the system which decrees that only one of them can float on the lake. I'm talking about a new system in which they can both float on the lake when they wish. It's not as though there isn't enough room for both of them.'

'I'd be out of a job, then,' he said, flippantly.

'That's not necessarily true. Even if they can both float right across to the other side without interruption they'll still need someone to bring them back here.'

'Alright,' he laughed. 'But how is the system going to be replaced?'

'It already has been replaced. I came here with the aim of destroying the system and that aim is all but fulfilled ... What I did first was to convince Miriam that I was on her side entirely, that I thought Rosa ought to die. Then this afternoon, after the failure of Miriam's pathetic plot to get you to row Rosa into range, I told her that tonight she would have her opportunity to lodge a bullet in Rosa's heart. I told her that I would come over here and prevent you from rescuing Rosa. I convinced her that there'd be no chance of me failing to do this. You were new to the job; you were weaker than me. I said that if I didn't convince you of the inevitability of Rosa's death I would break your arms instead. Then, as you know, I got you to get Rosa out of the way. After I'd jumped from the boat I swam about the lake for a while before going out and floating into range. Then I took the bullet meant for Rosa. So Miriam thinks that Rosa is dead. If my plan has worked she'll no longer be afraid of the water. If it has worked she'll be here any time now.'

Wilf shook his head slowly.

She's just demonstrated how many layers of falsehood she's capable of, he thought. How do I know this isn't another layer? Why should it be? What would be the point of another layer? Isn't this enough? I hope it's enough. I hope it's true. But what about the bullet? Is she above nature? Can she take a bullet like an ordinary person takes a blast of air?

'How did you take the bullet?' he said out loud.

'Simple,' she replied, grinning. 'I had a breastplate on. I knew she wouldn't miss the target, and the target was covered with metal.'

Wilf laughed. A breastplate. Whatever next? But the explanation satisfied him, even though he didn't quite believe it, even though he felt it might well be a disguise for the real explanation, which was perhaps too subtle to put into words.

Outside, a dog began to bark: a rhythmic, monotonous bark which gave the impression of being more of a signal than an attempt to frighten. Which dog could it be but the white dog? To whom could the barks refer but Miriam?

'Go and look,' said Magda. 'See for yourself that I've been telling you the truth.'

She motioned towards the window. He went over, opened the window, and stepped out onto the balcony. The moon was bright now. He could see the white dog, barking on the edge of the lake. Beyond that he could see a rowing boat with someone sitting in it: he couldn't tell whether it was Miriam or not. The person in the boat lifted something up and pointed it at the dog. The dog barked. A shot cracked out. The dog barked again. The gun was lowered for a while and then raised again. Another shot. The dog carried on with his barking as though nothing had happened.

Wilf stepped back into the room:

'There's someone in a boat shooting at the dog, but it can't be Miriam – unless she's aiming to miss.'

Magda grinned:

'She won't be aiming to miss. It's the dog, you see. The purity of the dog presents no target. She can't hit him.'

Rosa burst into the room.

'What's happening?' she shouted. 'There's someone

shooting at the dog. Who is it? Who can it be?'

She turned and spoke directly to Magda:

'You're behind this, aren't you?'

'It's Miriam,' said Magda, coolly. 'She thinks she has shot you. She believes you are dead. She's no longer afraid of the water.'

Rosa was silent for a long time after this wave had broken over her. She didn't move. Her face gave no indication of what she was feeling.

I bet she's mad, thought Wilf. I bet she's already trying to work out how she can get rid of Miriam. She'll probably set the dog on her and have done with it.

He was judging her, assuming that pride was her salient characteristic, assuming that she'd do anything rather than share her sovereignty of the lake.

Eventually she walked slowly over and sat down on the edge of the bed.

'Miriam? Down there, on the water?' she said.

Magda nodded.

'She's on the water, and I'm still alive. I never thought it was possible ... You've committed a miracle.'

She stared at the floor. She screwed up her eyes. She looked afraid.

'I'm still alive but the world I was living in has died and a different world has been born. I'm the same person in a different world, so I'm lost. I don't know which way to go. I don't know how to react.'

'But you are a different person,' said Magda. 'You've already reacted. You want to be told what to do. When did someone last tell you what to do? Where's all your pride gone?'

'Yes,' said Rosa, looking round as though pride was an autonomous entity. 'Where has it gone?'

'I'll tell you what to do, if you like,' said Magda. 'I'll tell you the only thing you can do: accept Miriam as your equal, your sister. Share the lake and the house with her.'

Rosa stood up; walked quickly across the room and back; stared at Wilf; stared at Magda. The solemnity of her expression was suddenly usurped by a smile.

'Yes!' she exclaimed, exultantly. 'Why not? Why not? ... Just think what could be achieved. I've lost half the rights to the lake and I've gained all the rights to all the lake.'

So I was wrong, thought Wilf. Unless she's pretending. But what about me? What'll happen to me?

'Wait a minute,' said Rosa. 'If Miriam sees me now isn't she likely to relapse into her prevoius state?'

'It's possible,' said Magda. 'I think it would be best if you went to bed and left it to me.'

'Alright,' said Rosa.

She turned to Wilf:

'If you go down to the jetty and ask Miriam to land, the dog will stop barking and retire. He knows that you wouldn't do anything that I didn't want you to do.'

'O.K.,' said Wilf.

He walked along to the end of the jetty. Miriam was sitting motionlessly in the boat, gazing down at the water.

'You can land now,' he called to her. 'The dog won't touch you.'

And indeed, as soon as he had spoken the dog stopped barking and walked away into the darkness of the wood. Miriam rowed the boat to the jetty and got out, leaving the rifle behind. Her hair and clothes were wet.

'Hello,' she said, beaming at him. 'How's your arm?'

'Alright.'

'Did Magda send you down?'

'Yes.'

'So here I am,' she said. 'My lake, my jetty, my land, my house, my lake.'

'Yes,' he agreed. 'It's amazing what a bullet can buy these days.'

'Not that I need it all myself,' she said. 'That was just the way it had to be.'

'I see,' said Wilf.

'I never really thought it would happen,' she confided. 'Although I thought of it as a purpose, I never really thought of it as the sort of purpose which could be achieved. And I never would have achieved it on my own, I realise that now. It's only thanks to Magda ... How did she manage to prevent you from rescuing Rosa?'

'Persuaded me that Rosa's death was inevitable.'

'Ah, yes.'

As far as she's concerned she's a murderess, thought Wilf. Doesn't she feel any remorse about putting another person to death? Doesn't she feel any fear about the consequences?

'What about the law?' he said. 'You must realise that what you've done is against the law. If the law finds out it'll be down on you like a ton of bricks.'

She kept on smiling.

'The law won't find out. It hasn't got eyes for acts such as mine. It wasn't a crime. It was an act of justice.'

'What if I tell the police?' he suggested.

'You'd be wasting your time.'

She gestured towards the lake.

'Where's the body? There is no body. Rosa's body has dissolved. It is everywhere. All over the lake.'

'Oh, yes? How come it's dissolved, then?'

'It dissolved because after it was dead it didn't need to carry on pretending that it was any different from the water which surrounded it.'

'I see,' he said, ironically. 'So you don't feel any remorse about having killed her?'

'None whatsoever,' she replied. 'My cause was just. It was my birthright to do what I did, and what's more she knew it. And anyway, what has she lost by it. Nothing, not even her body. Her body is with her wherever she goes.'

She began to walk towards the house. Wilf stared at the version of the moon which undulated beneath the water, then he turned and followed her. He was glad Rosa wasn't dead. If she'd been dead he'd have had a difficult decision to make. As it was, he could just follow whatever path was opened up to him.

After they'd got into the house she had a quick look into the downstairs rooms before asking where Magda was. He led her upstairs. Magda was still lying in his bed. Miriam embraced her with exclamations of gratitude and joy.

'But what are you doing in bed? Aren't you well?' she asked, anxiously. 'Your dress is wet and torn. What's happened to you?'

'Sit down and I'll tell you,' said Magda. 'But wouldn't you like to change your clothes first? You must be cold.'

'No, no,' said Miriam. 'I want to keep these clothes on. It's a luxury for me to be wet.'

She squatted down beside the bed. Wilf sat down in the armchair.

'After I'd persuaded Wilf here that Rosa's death was inevitable I decided to take the boat out and make sure that your bullet struck home,' said Magda. 'It wasn't that I doubted your marksmanship. It was just that I felt something might happen after the bullet had left the gun which would prevent it from entering Rosa's heart.'

'Like what?' said Miriam, laughing. 'What could happen?'

'Any number of things could have appeared and acted as shields or deflectors. It wouldn't have been at all surprising. You can never be absolutely sure about inevitability, can you? And of course if her death hadn't been inevitable then all the forces in the area would have been concentrated upon producing a shield to prevent the bullet from striking home. But as you know my doubts weren't vindicated. The colours went out from her as soon as you'd fired your shot. She was left in darkness. I rowed up to her and saw that the hole in her wet-suit was perfectly placed. Her eyes were open; her limbs motionless. She was dead. I heard you shouting as you ran down to the water. I waited for her body to dissolve, but it didn't do so. It didn't even sink. I decided to bring her back to land and bury her in the woods somewhere. I leaned out of the boat and took hold of her beneath her armpits. The next thing I knew her hands were gripping my neck; I was being pulled into the water; the boat was capsizing; she was screaming. I fought with her in the water for a long time. Her strength and savagery were amazing, but eventually I managed to knock her out. Then I swam back here with her and Wilf and I brought her in.'

Miriam looked horrified. She slumped down onto the floor.

'So she isn't dead, then?' she said.

'Who isn't dead?' said Magda, laughing. 'The Rosa you wanted to kill, the Rosa you had to kill, is dead. I told you that. As dead as a doorknob. You know it yourself anyway. You know better than anyone how dead she is. If you hadn't killed her you wouldn't have lost your fear of the water, would you?'

'No, I suppose not,' admitted Miriam.

She brightened up a little.

'But who is it, then?' she asked. 'Who is it that's alive? Where is she?'

'She's in bed in the next room. Her name is Rosa. Her appearance isn't a great deal different from the appearance of the other Rosa, but she's certainly a different person: she's perfectly prepared to share everything with you – the lake, the house, the dog, the land, everything. She's perfectly prepared to be your sister. Isn't she, Wilf?'

'Yes, it's true,' agreed Wilf.

'But how did it happen?' asked Miriam. 'How did this resurrection come about?'

'I don't know,' said Magda. 'I can only conjecture that she had got herself into such a fluid state that her heart and her ribs and her skin were able to reform soon after the bullet had passed through them. And they reformed around a new person. It's obvious you can't die and be reborn as the same person. It's obvious that if you die you must be reborn as a different person, even though as in a case like this you are reborn into the same body as the previous person had occupied. Anyway, whatever has happened has happened. There are two holes in her wet-suit, and no marks on her skin ...'

That's it, thought Wilf. She's got it all sown up.

He found this new description of what had happened to Rosa more elegant and attractive than the one furnished by his memory. But he supposed that it could only be true if he'd spent the greater part of the evening dreaming; otherwise, its value must be purely symbolic.

Miriam stood up, smiling.

'Everything's alright, then,' she declared. 'I never wanted to have it all to myself anyway. I just presumed that was the way it would have to be.'

She stretched her body and sighed:

'I'm unbelievably tired. I must go to bed. I want to be fresh for the morning.'

She turned to Wilf:

'Which room shall I take?'

He shrugged:

'Any one you like, I should think – apart from the one next door.'

She smiled:

'Goodnight, then. Thankyou both.'
She went out.

Wilf picked up the black dress and inspected it. He found two small, round holes – one at the front and one at the back.

'Your breastplate wasn't very efficient,' he said.

'It did its job,' she replied.

He sat down on the bed and gazed at her. He saw her in a new light, an inconceivable light. She ought to be dead and she wasn't. The expansion of his universe had accelerated suddenly.

She pushed back the covers, baring her breasts. He leaned down and placed his lips upon the white place where the bullet would have entered. He felt the tolling of her heart. She moaned with apparent pleasure. He parted his lips and pressed his tongue against her.

He wasn't asking for anything, he wasn't sucking, and yet he felt an influx from this contact; something came into him which seemed capable of erasing the shadows in his mind.

But now she moaned again, and this time it seemed to him that she was expressing pain rather than pleasure. He raised his head so that he could see into her eyes.

'What's the matter?' he asked, frowning.

She smiled and nodded towards her chest. He looked down and saw a little disc of blood on the place where he had kissed her. He wiped his mouth and tongue, thinking or rather hoping that the blood was his. But his hand was clear: the blood must have appeared since he lifted his head: the blood must have come from within her.

You've opened her wound, he thought. She's had it now. You've taken her life away from her. You've got her life inside you. How could I have her life inside me? It doesn't make sense. But it's here all around you. I can see it and feel it and hear it. It's telling me that it's here, and I'm telling you.

'What's happened?' he said out loud.

'The truth's come out,' she replied. 'You've got it. I can do without it.'

'I'll get a doctor,' he said, half-heartedly.

'Don't be fatuous.'

The disc of blood was gradually expanding.

I'll stem it with my tongue, he thought. My tongue opened it; my tongue can close it.

He leaned down, but she pushed him away with her hand.

'You can't give me anything,' she said. 'Some processes are irreversible. Don't worry about it. I'm not worried about it. It isn't even particularly painful.'

He began to accept that nothing could be done.

But has it always been inevitable? he thought. Or am I responsible? If I'd carried on believing that she'd used a breastplate, would she have carried on living? If I hadn't looked at the dress; if I hadn't found the two holes; if I hadn't kissed her there; would she still be alright? If you hadn't kissed her there you wouldn't have been born.

'Don't think about it, Wilf. I'm alright. I did what I set out to do. I don't need to be alive any more. You can have my life if you want it. If you take it then all three of you will have gained something and I'll have lost nothing I'm particularly fond of. What could be better than that?'

Wilf grinned, almost chuckled.

Why not? he thought. Why not see things the way she draws them? If I see them like that now then when she's gone I'll be able to draw them like that for myself. Perhaps that's what she means when she says she's offering me her life. By taking her life I won't have killed her, I'll have accepted her. I can choose to let her voice take the place of those other voices, or I can let her die within me. But if I let her die I'll have to forget her entirely. She's too inconceivable to be an object in my memory; she's too inconceivable to be anything but a subject ...

His thoughts bumbled on in this fashion for a while longer, only stopping when they began to bite their own tails.

Magda took hold of his hand.

'If anything goes wrong with them tomorrow morning you'll make it right, won't you?'

'Yes,' he said, softly. 'Of course I will.'

She inspired him. What had inspired her?

'I know what you've done,' he said. 'I know how you

did it. But I don't know why you did it. What motivated
you in the first place?'

'Who can tell?' she said.

There was mirth in her eyes.

'Perhaps it was the lake which motivated me. Perhaps it
was my own liberty. I was fluid, while Rosa and Miriam
were transfixed by a system which was as rigid as it was
absurd. Rosa couldn't achieve half of what she wanted to
achieve and Miriam couldn't achieve anything at all. It was
no bother for me to move out of the frame of thinking that
the system was necessary because it had always existed and
into the frame of thinking that it was unnecessary because it
had never existed.'

Her voice had become noticeably fainter. The blood had
begun to run down over her ribs. She seemed to be coming
towards him and going away from him at the same time.
She groaned, but the smile didn't leave her eyes. He wanted
to weep, yet he knew that it would be both pointless and
insulting.

'There must be something I can do,' he cried, despite
himself.

'One thing,' she murmured. 'Take me down to the
lake.'

He began to protest.

'Take me now,' she ordered.

He wrapped her dress around her. Then he picked her up
and carried her out.

The lake was calm. The moon was out in force. The white
dog was sitting at the water's edge, perhaps waiting to bear
witness to what was going to happen.

She seemed lighter than she ought to have been: she was
no strain on his muscles. He felt he could have held her
until the birds began to sing; longer, if necessary.

'Put me into the water,' she said.

He tightened his clasp upon her.

This is ridiculous, he thought. No. It's what she needs.
Who are you to deny her? Who are you to deny yourself?

He walked into the water and put her down.

She sighed with relief.

'The pain's gone already,' she said.

He nodded.

'In a few minutes there'll be no evidence of me outside yourself,' she said.

Then she winked at him. She winked an enormous, comical wink which involved the whole of her face. This wink punctured the sorrow which had been inflating inside him. This wink changed his mind. Now he knew for certain that she wasn't leaving him at all. Her blackness and her whiteness had already begun to drift away, but her colours were safely enveloped by his skin.

The dog stood up and went back into the wood, as if satisfied by what had taken place. Wilf walked lightly back up to his room. His own satisfaction was sealed when he saw that the sheet on his bed bore no trace of blood.

III
TWO STORIES

Copi

Translated by John Calder and John Gallienne

Photograph of Copi by Jerry Bauer

Copi (who uses no first name) was born in the Argentine in 1939 but has made his reputation in France as a cartoonist, designer, actor, playwright and novelist. Four of his plays are published by John Calder (Publishers) Ltd as *Eva Peron* and other plays. His novel *Drag Ball* will be published in 1981. These two stories first appeared in Hara Kiri in Paris and were published by Christian Bourgois under the title Une Langouste pour Deux.

THE GOYA SELF-PORTRAIT

The Duchess of Alba was so thin that she was frequently referred to inelegantly as "the skeleton"; this was made even more humiliating as her younger sister, the Duchess of Malaga, who was reputed to be the most beautiful woman in Spain, had turned the heads of several crowned heads up to the moment when, on reaching her majority and having to decide between three young kings, she quietly announced that she was entering a convent. The family of the two young duchesses, in spite of its piety, was thrown into consternation. The old Count of Salamanca entertained a passion for his younger daughter who resembled her dead mother, dead in childbirth, as closely as two drops of water, whereas the Duchess of Alba was the very picture of her father who had been nicknamed "the vulture" in all the courts of Europe, so repulsive was his ugliness. Don Jose Ignacio (as he was called) even threatened to kill himself with his revolver if his younger daughter were to enter holy orders.

The Duchess of Alba supported her sister's vocation with tenacity; she passed whole nights enclosed in the library with her father, talking to him softly but firmly of God and the will of their mother in heaven, until she touched the heart of the old man who finally agreed. The Duchess of Malaga went through the iron grilles of a Carmelite convent and the heavy door closed behind her. The old Count sobbed convulsively, leaning on the shoulder of his elder daughter whose aquiline profile was now lit up by a pious smile. Thereafter Don Jose Ignacio allowed despair to take over; he had no longer any taste for anything at all and relinquished himself to death assisted and perhaps even helped by the negligence of the Duchess of Alba, who one night put too much belladonna into the cup of lime tea that she usually brought him at midnight while he dozed on his pillows with the original parchment edition of Don Quixote in his hands, his reading glasses resting on the end of his nose. The Duchess of Malaga came out of the Carmelite convent one last time to take part in Don Jose Ignacio's funeral service in the Cathedral of Toledo at which practically all the crowned heads of Europe were present. Just at the moment when the two sisters were sinking onto their knees for the *Te Deum*, the young King of Spain cried out to the Duchess of Malaga, "I love you!" and threw himself at her feet. The Duchess of Malaga immediately rose, left the church, entered a carriage and disappeared forever behind the doors of the convent.

The Duchess of Alba found herself at the age of 21 in possession of 43 duchies and 17 counties, with five castles in the four corners of Spain and the most famous bullring in Andalusia, and with her sister bound by vows of total abstinence. She naturally had to wear mourning for a year, entertaining seldom and then only a few intimates of noble family to whom she offered sumptuous dinners at which she herself ate like an ogre, but without ever increasing her weight above her normal 39 kilos, consisting entirely of nerves and bone. She tried on several occasions to get to know the aristocratic young men that she met at coronations and marriages better, but her ugliness created only a circle of cold air about her; in the official group photographs, in spite of her nobility from a very ancient line, she was always pushed back to the last row and hidden behind the hat of the Queen Mother of Greece. Little by little she retired to her castle on the Escurial, not daring to go out in Madrid except in a carriage equipped with dark glass, so much did she fear the taunts of the children of the street, pityless towards her ugliness. The old nobles that she received there were the friends of her father and as ugly as herself: the old Conte des Asturias who was covered with boils, and the Duke of Castile, her Godfather, who was a hunchback.

The Duke of Castile met a young man at one of his Cousins' houses, a tennis champion and an Argentinian; he decided to invite him to supper with the Duchess of Alba, thinking that his Goddaughter never saw anyone except the boring and the old. Prince Florencio Goyete Solis, coming from minor nobility, born in the Argentine, son of Prince Goyete and a descendant of Aztec nobility, had kept, despite his 45 years, a young smile, a bronzed skin, a necklace of seals' teeth, dark glasses, and a yachting cap. He was delighted to be received by the Duchess of Alba, knowing of her considerable fortune and extreme piety (he had been told that she slept on her knees on a *prie-dieu*) and also of the numerous misfortunes that had struck her honourable family. But he was also curious to see the Duchess because of her ugliness, reputed to be the most frightening in European nobility.

Florencio entered an immense Andalusian patio where the Duchess of Alba received him almost hidden by the shade of a jasmin tree, her face obscured by a black mantilla. They moved immediately to table. This was covered with a great variety of grilled meats and lit by a single candle. Florencio sat between the Count of Asturias and the Duke of Castille and the Duchess established herself at the far end of the table. Florencio gradually accustomed his eyes sufficiently well to the reigning gloom to be able to make out the face of the Duchess who, from time to time, would quickly raise a corner of the mantilla that hid her face and put a large piece of meat into her mouth with the help of a silver fork. The impression finally created by the Duchess of Alba was, in the last resort, not so much of ugliness, but of extreme emaciation, with her skin glued to her skull, of her very dark eyes sunk into the back of their orbits, of the prominence of her teeth and the pale greyness of her skin. She pronounced not a single word during dinner, being too occupied in devouring, all by herself, an almost raw sucking pig in less than forty minutes, while the others talked about the Hohenzollern dynasty to which Florencio belonged through an alliance of his mother. When they had passed into the drawing room where two candles discreetly illuminated Goya's *Maja Vestida* and *Maja Desnuda*, the celebrated portraits of a celebrated earlier Duchess of Alba, ancestress of the present one, the Conte de la Castile and the Duke of Asturias excused themselves rapidly, put on their capes and left in their carriages, while Florencio accepted a final glass of sherry before listening to the Duchess's orchestra, 30 guitars arranged around the patio. The two old Dukes

congratulated themselves on their initiative; they believed
that they had noticed in the slightly slower movements of
the Duchess signs of a certain interest and the young man
seemed to them to be very well behaved; the Duchess of
Alba could not hope for even the most minor European
betrothal because of her looks, so why not turn to the
Argentine nobility which dubious though it might be, was
to be found more and more often in Spain? The Duchess of
Alba wrapped herself in a mantilla coat, asked her guest to
take a chair in the middle of the patio and placed herself
three steps behind him in the shade of a magnolia. The
guitarists, all of them blind, had been positioned around
the patio by the old butler who looked like one of Goya's
monsters; for the moment he appeared to be the only
servant in this immense castle. They played a cante-jondo
while a blind old man threw out lamentations such as
would give anyone goose pimples; this continued for a good
hour.

The Argentinian gigolo watched the Duchess from the
corner of his eye as she sat stiff and immobile under her
mantilla. For the first time in his life he felt intimidated by a
woman. Florencio Goyete Solis had been the tennis
champion of his club in the southern suburb of Buenas
Aires. His youthful notoriety had brought him a good
marriage to the daughter of an industrialist, a
manufacturer of tennis rackets. Then Peron came to power
(this was in 1945) and the industrialist and his family were
ruined. Florencio divorced to follow a Brazilian widow to
Rio, then he found an American lady, then went on to a
Venezuelian with whom he spent ten years, but who finally
threw him off her yacht at Torremolinos with a cheque for a
thousand dollars and his suitcases. That was a year ago. He
had tried to introduce himself into all the salons of Spain,
but Spanish women were not easy; either they were too
prudish or much too poor. It was much the same in
Argentina; one had to get married. But at 45 years old one
could not hope for an heiress when one only had a dubious
title of nobility and a tennis racket; the Duchess of Alba
was the only real chance that had presented itself to him
since his arrival in Spain. He decided therefore to "play it
tight" as the Argentinians say. He rose from his black
bamboo armchair, rebuttoned his blue blazer and going up

to the Duchess bowed low, asking her "Would you like to dance, Duchess?" The Duchess stayed for a moment perplexed. She had never danced in her life, nor ever seen anyone dance, except in films. The only music that she believed to be proper was the cante-jondo. But that one listened to, one did not dance to it. She liked religious music, but only at early masses at dawn. The Argentinian prince seemed to her to be out of place; he had a yachting cap instead of a crown and a tennis racket instead of a sceptre. She had only invited him to listen to her evening cante-jondo out of simple politeness for the Duke of Castile who had invited him, but she did not feel herself in any way attracted by the parody of authentic monarchy that this Creole prince only knew through photographs in the more sordid social chronicles. "I do not dance, please sit down," she said to him in a dry voice. He sat down again and patiently awaited the end of the cante-jondo, but let the Duchess know through the discreet tap of his foot on the ground, that he would have preferred a less formal contact. In addition, the heat was oppressive; he slowly opened his white silk scarf. The hum of the crickets nearly drowned out the cante-jondo.

Suddenly a flash of lightning appeared in the sky. Florencio took advantage of it to glance at the Duchess and was appalled by her cadaverous expression but told himself that it was probably an effect created by the lightning. A strong wind suddenly rose, the lights went out and it started to pour in buckets. Florencio threw himself on to the Duchess who was rolling, pushed by the wind, over the ground which was now transformed into a mass of debris. She was practically fainting from the shock. He raised her like a feather in his large arms and moved towards the drawing room where the two trembling candles continued to flicker before the two majas. He closed the door to the veranda. Outside, the old blind players twanged away, pulling at the watery strings while one lightning flash succeeded another. Florencio Goyete Solis deposited the fainting Duchess of Alba onto the divan, the same one, he suddenly noticed, as in the two paintings. He brought one of the candalabra up to the divan where the duchess was lying just as she returned to consciousness. She hiccupped, then proceeded to throw up onto the floor the whole sucking pig that she had eaten at dinner. She then said to him, "Is that you, Prince Solis? Come a little closer." He sat down on the corner of the divan, fighting against the nausea caused by the smell of the vomit. The Duchess squeezed his hand so hard that it hurt and asked him, "Help me to get up." He helped her. "That way," she said, pointing her crooked finger towards an enormous door. Florencio helped her to walk as far as the door and opened it: inside was an enormous library, even larger than the patio, with parchments pressed together on the shelves, rising up to the ceiling which was over thirteen feet high. The old monster of a butler lit a candalabra every ten yards. At the end was an enormous desk behind which loomed a black chair in carved wood nine feet high, onto which the old ogre of a butler then climbed in order to illuminate a portrait hung high up on the wall, after which he disappeared through a trap-door. The Duchess of Alba recovered her aplomb well enough to take Florencio by the arm and lead him slowly through the library as far as the desk. Left and right, the paintings of Goya hung on the walls. "That is Goya's self-portrait as a young man," she said, pointing to the portrait behind the black chair. Florencio could not believe his eyes: the self-portrait was as like himself as two peas in a pod: the shape of the face, the moustache, the expression, it was him. He turned to look at the Duchess of Alba who was smiling at him with all her gold teeth and all her gums. "You will paint my portrait," she said and let her mantilla fall to the ground so that he could see her spindly arms. She undressed, which took some time because of the number of underclothes that hid her skeletal body. Florencio Goyete Solis sank heavily onto the black chair and lit a cigar. By a strange accident he had achieved the limit of his ambitions. He would marry the Duchess and then get rid of her. Nobody would be surprised if this female hunchback of thirty-nine kilos were to die in childbirth, after, naturally, he had played the part of the loving husband for two or three years.

The Duchess of Alba felt herself to be transformed by some kind of miracle, imagining that she had taken on the body and the face of her sister, the beautiful Duchess of Malaga, cloistered in her convent. She kept her naked body draped in her black mantilla as she prudishly approached

Florencio, and then jumped suddenly onto his fly which she opened with one sudden movement and then took his sex into her mouth. Being absolutely ignorant of the facts of life she thought that it was in this way that women were impregnated. Florencio closed his eyes and tried to think of a young girl from the suburbs of Buenas Aires who during all his childhood had given him an erection at a mere glance, but he felt that his penis was still soft. The Duchess of Alba was chewing him too hard. He tried with his hand to delicately relax the Duchess' face, a gesture which caused her mantilla and her wig to fall off. The Duchess of Alba had a sensation of pleasure for the first time in her life and clenched her teeth together. Florencio screamed, jumped six feet away and threw himself against the window of the library. He went right through the glass, falling onto a bed of carnations under the beating rain, bleeding from the gaping hole where the Duchess had bitten off his sex with her teeth. He had one last pious thought of his mother, then cried out loud, "What a thing to happen, what a thing ..." and died.

Translated by John Calder

TRUDY LORELEI

Trudy Lorelei sat angrily on her rucksack. She had missed her train to Loir-et-Cher. She had bought a French style lollipop, a very small one, with serrated edges. The Gare de Lyon made her want to puke, it was so polluted, and then there were the blacks who drove around the station in machines like lawn-mowers, only very fast, as if they wanted to run you over. She had to get to the American Express in Loir-et-Cher before closing time. All she had left were two one dollar bills, three notes of ten francs each together with a few tokens for the telephone, the whole lot stuffed into the back pocket of her jeans. Among the tokens was a French one and to pass the time she decided to ring a French girl she'd met in Amsterdam.

She hoisted her rucksack back onto her shoulders and set off towards the phone booths. One of those monstrous lawn-mower machines knocked into her and the black man who was driving it shouted something at her she didn't understand. She teetered under the weight of her rucksack, lost her balance and keeled over, banging her knee on the ground. She was asking herself whether she should make a complaint, as she would have done in the United States, when an old gentleman resembling Charles Boyer helped her to her feet. '*Merci*,' she said in the best French she could manage, and continued limping towards the phone booths. Having dumped her rucksack on the ground, she dialled the number. Trudy was very large, and had very long and fine frizzy blonde hair, done in afro-style; her eye make-up was very black and she was wearing a jeans suit with black clogs, her full lips painted a crimson red. Françoise's number was engaged. The gentleman resembling Charles Boyer was looking at her through the glass door of the booth; he had followed her.

She dialled the number again. It rang. 'Hello, Françoise, it's me, Trudy Lorelei!' There was a silence at the other end of the line, then Françoise's voice: 'Trudy, *darling*, where are you?' 'I'm at the Gare de Lyon!' said Trudy. 'Ring me next time you're in Paris.' said Françoise's voice and rang off. Trudy was shocked. She had put up Françoise for a week in Amsterdam, they had dropped acid together, and Françoise had wanted to throw herself out the window, because her photographer husband had slept with a German transvestite. Trudy had caught hold of her on the window ledge just in time and had talked to her all through the night, comforting her as best she could with her handful of French words. Françoise had left the next morning, stealing two fifty dollar bills and leaving the door unlocked. Trudy had been angry for a few days, but then thought that Françoise needed the money more than she did; and little by little she had begun to admire the courage of this young Frenchwoman who had, without realising it, married a homosexual, brought up her three-year-old daughter single handed in a small bed-sit by giving tap-dancing lessons, with numerous fits of depression when she couldn't get pupils and with a landlady who wanted to kick her out because the little girl cried at night, while all the time remaining faithful to her husband, hoping that he would come back to her. But her husband had hennaed his hair and covered himself with sequins and then gone off to start a new life in Amsterdam. Françoise had left Paris to look for him one last time, intending to implore him to stay with her and with their little daughter, but he had slapped her in public at the opening of an art exhibition where Trudy Lorelei happened to be present; it was Trudy who had aroused all the women artists present to throw the young husband out of the gallery. Young Françoise at the time was sobbing in a corner between two green plastic statues. The women artists clustered round her, took her up immediately, and it was Trudy who took Françoise home to sleep in her room.

Through the glass door of the phone booth Trudy saw the old man who resembled Charles Boyer still standing there looking at her. He took a banana out of his mackintosh pocket, peeled it like a monkey and proceeded to eat it. Trudy wondered what she could do for the next hour; she thought she would very much like a sandwich, even if there was no ketchup, and set off slowly towards the café. She asked for *'Un sandwich, Mademoiselle.'* It was practically all she could say in French, so she said it with a great deal of conviction. 'Paté, sausage, potted meat, camembert, gruyère?' 'Camembert!' said Trudy, who detested Camembert, but it was the only word she had understood and, more importantly, she thought it would be the cheapest. The old gentleman resembling Charles Boyer came and sat at the bar next to her. The barmaid said to him 'Well, if it isn't Monsieur Boyer, s'a long time since we last saw you.' She gave Trudy her sandwich, who took out a ten franc note. Monsieur Boyer swallowed a glass of Cotes-du-Rhone, talking all the while to the barmaid. Trudy didn't understand a word of the conversation; she bit into her sandwich with rage, she was furious with Françoise. She had planned to pick up her allowance from the American Express in Loir-et-Cher, come back to Paris and rent an attic studio with Françoise and her little girl in order to learn French. Then she was counting on going back to the U.S.A. to give French classes at the University of Maryland; together with Françoise, of course. She told herself it was stupid to get so worked up about this rude and pretentious young Frenchwoman. With the money she'd be picking up, she could spend the summer in Greece.

The waitress gave her the change; she had devoured her sandwich without noticing it. The old gentleman resembling Charles Boyer pinched her left buttock which made her jump and she dropped the saucer of change which rolled to the ground. The sadistic old man burst out laughing, so, too, did the woman behind the counter. When Trudy bent down to pick up her change, he slapped her buttocks, and several customers, leaning on their elbows at the bar, laughed as well. Trudy shouted 'You pig! Pig!' at the old man, picked up her rucksack and without looking back marched out into the main concourse; the whole restaurant burst out laughing as she tripped over the doorstep and landed in a heap on the ground. One of the machines that looked like a Walt Disney train nearly ran her down. The black man who drove it was laughing; he turned the machine round and bore down on her again. She had the presence of mind to fling herself back inside the café, banging her head against the glass door. The machine bowled over her rucksack and out tumbled T-shirts, a pair of heeled sandals, an Indian scarf. The gentleman resembling Charles Boyer rushed to her aid. He made her sit down on a chair and undid the jacket of her jeans suit, exposing her huge breasts, blotched with red. The old woman from behind the bar arrived with a compress of ice cubes wrapped in a napkin, which she pressed against the bump on Trudy's forehead while the black man charged at the café window, shattering it to fragments. The customers within panicked and fled to the street exit, while the black reversed and charged again at the gaping hole in the window. The machine burst into the café and bore down on Trudy knocking over tables and chairs.

The gentleman resembling Charles Boyer pulled a revolver from his pocket and fired at the black, who fell to the tiled floor. The machine smashed through the street window and began to run amok in front of the station. Trudy stood up as best she could; her leg hurt her very badly, the machine had given her a great bruise on the ankle, and she had lost her clogs. Then the police arrived, and the man resembling Charles Boyer took Trudy by the arm, forcing her into the lavatories just as the tear gas grenades burst inside the café. Trudy caught a glimpse of the customers hiding behind the bar and slinging bottles at the police. The gentleman resembling Charles Boyer pointed the revolver at her and said 'Drop your knickers!' Without understanding the words, Trudy grasped the meaning of the gesture and did so. The old man slapped her, forced her to her knees, and after having struck her on the head with the gun, forced it into her anus; it hurt her terribly, but she didn't make a sound for fear that the old man might pull the trigger. With his free hand he masturbated, and just as he was starting to gasp the police banged loudly at the door. He quickly thrust the revolver into his pocket and pushed his penis back under his mac. Trudy was trembling with fear, crouched over the lavatory bowl from which the old man had forced her to drink urine; her face and her beautiful blonde hair were coated with excrement; she instinctively pulled up her jeans just as the old man opened the door to the police, saying 'Here she is, gentlemen, I have arrested her!' And he held out the revolver to one of the cops. Another flung himself on Trudy,

dragging her outside, while a third hand-cuffed her. They
got her out of the café very quickly and the hub-bub
stopped at once. All the windows had been shattered, even
the mirrors, as had the china and the bottles. The tables
and chairs had been overturned, several people had been
injured by splinters of glass; an ambulance was taking
away a score of them. The body of the black man lay on a
bench in the middle of the room, a fine rivulet of blood
trickling from his mouth. A policeman covered him with a
checked table cloth. The *patronne* rushed at Trudy shouting
'Murderer! Murderer!' while a hundred people massed in
the station concourse began to shout 'Kill her! Kill her!' A
cordon of police tried to keep them out of the cafeteria.

Amongst the cries from the crowd, Trudy distinctly
heard several times the word 'guillotine', one of the very few
she knew in French. She began to shout 'Help! Help!
Help!' and tried to clear herself a path towards the
ambulance, but the nurses pushed her back, one of them
hitting her in the face with her fist, another kicking her on
the knee, and the cops took her away just as the crowd's
attacks were becoming dangerous. While two of them hit
her with truncheons, the others did the same to a growing
number of people who wanted to lynch her. With her jacket
torn to shreds, she was thrust into a Black Maria which was
locked with a loud crash. She found herself, covered in
bruises, on the floor of the van which the crowd was rocking
in an effort to overturn it. She managed to drag herself to
one of the grilles in the Black Maria to look outside. The
cops had their weapons trained on the civilians who were
standing facing the station wall, their hands behind their
heads. Several children were crying and running hither and
thither. Old Monsieur Boyer went from one group of cops
to the next giving orders. The black's corpse was brought
out on a stretcher by two cops, they opened the Black
Maria and pushed it in. Trudy, terrified, huddled at the
back of the van. Having dropped the corpse heavily on the
floor, the two cops got out again and closed the door.
Outside, Monsieur Boyer was giving instructions with a
loud hailer, the crowd was dispersing and the cops were
getting back into their vans. The *patronne* of the cafeteria set
fire to a dish-rag and threw it into the vehicle Trudy was in.
A fireman sprayed it briefly with his hose, until the Black

Maria was inundated with water. Trudy got a jet full in the face, she was coughing, the smoke was suffocating her, and she tried to find refuge close to the ground, side by side with the black man's corpse, where the smoke was less thick.

Suddenly, the vehicle started while sirens wailed. The smoke dispersed enough for Trudy to be able to drag herself to the rear grille. Monsieur Boyer was following her, driving a black limousine. Two lines of speed cops protected the motorcade from the wrath of the crowd, massed on the pavements along their route. The word 'guillotine' was more and more firmly chanted. Trudy gripped the bars and shouted 'Help! Help! Help!' as loud as she could. The Black Maria turned, braking harshly, and Trudy fell over on top of the black's corpse, clinging to it instinctively. Outside there was an enormous commotion; sirens, howls and whistle blasts merged into one another. The door of the Black Maria opened, and the old gentleman resembling Charles Boyer got in, then the Black Maria set off again. He sat down on a bench, took a transistor radio out of his pocket and listened to it attentively, without paying the least attention to Trudy. At last the vehicle stopped very gently amidst the pealing of bells. Monsieur Boyer took a comb from his pocket and combed his moustache just as the door opened, and Trudy, spellbound, saw the spire of the Sainte-Chapelle, which she had only previously known from postcards she had seen. She found herself within the walls of a square, grey building which encircled the courtyard where the Black Maria had come to a halt. The cops were setting up a guillotine in the courtyard. The gentleman resembling Charles Boyer got out of the van without looking at her and disappeared from view. She rushed to the side grille of the Black Maria to see a large crowd gathered in the courtyard, singing *La Carmagnole*, which she recognised, having heard it in a French film.

Behind the crowd and the six storey buildings, Trudy saw the twin towers of Notre Dame from which flew two tricolour flags standing out against the blue sky of a Sunday in May. An enormous man, with thick ginger moustaches, dressed like a French butcher, leapt into the Black Maria and slung the black man's corpse over his shoulder. He got out. Someone shut the door again. Trudy listened to the laughter of the crowd. Just now the cops were building a pyre in another corner of the courtyard. The butcher threw the black onto a wooden table, undressed him deftly, and began to dismember him using a variety of knives which a young blond boy sharpened as they were needed. That lasted a good while. The cops lit the pyre with charcoal; soon it was burning fiercely; the crowd shouted 'Bravo!' each time the butcher detached a limb from the black's corpse, which the apprentice would then throw onto the pyre. A smell of burnt meat filled the air while the crowd whooped like red Indians. The cops took pieces of the roast out of the fire and ran to pass them through the railings to the crowd. The black's corpse thus disappeared in a few minutes. Then, the butcher and the apprentice did a few pirouettes on their hands around the wooden table; the apprentice took a brand from the pyre and swallowed fire while dancing on the table, meanwhile the butcher covered his face with a black stocking with holes for his mouth, his moustache and his eyes and stationed himself, arms crossed at the top of the steps leading to the guillotine.

The crowd was shouting hysterically, Trudy was trembling with fear. She ran to the grille on the other side of the Black Maria to see the fireman's parade band coming down the Law Court steps playing the *Marseillaise*. Behind the firemen came two lines of old men covered in medals and, in the middle, dressed in a long black robe and wearing a curling, white wig on his head, was Monsieur Boyer with a pair of scales in his hand. At his appearance the crowd became delirious. Monsieur Boyer stopped at the top of the steps and silenced it with a gesture. He made a speech of which Trudy only understood two words which were repeated unceasingly: 'justice' and 'guillotine'. The railings gave way before the weight of the crowd. Hundreds of people invaded the courtyard, a number of youths wearing caps and scarves dragged and kicked Trudy out of the van. She stood up in pain and launched herself at a run towards the guillotine. She did not want to die at the hands of a lynch-mob. On the way people hit her, but she managed to drag herself to the foot of the scaffold.

The executioner helped her to climb the steps; then he kissed her full and long on the mouth, biting her lips savagely and squeezing her throat and the nape of her neck between his pincer-like fingers. Trudy hadn't an ounce of strength left in a single muscle; the executioner held her up by the hair like a puppet, despite her thirteen stone. The crowd burst out laughing, and threw paving stones at her. The young apprentice was busy sharpening the guillotine. The butcher put her head in the *lunette*, and she found herself staring at the weaving of the basket, saying 'It isn't true' at the moment the blade cut through her neck. In a last flash she saw the face of her mother, who had died in childbirth and whom she had only known from photographs. The crowd danced in a circle round the guillotine and the pyre, where a few children groped amongst the embers for the last of the black's bones to gnaw. Monsieur Boyer turned on his heel, climbed back up the steps to the Law Courts, whose heavy door he slammed behind him, abandoning the excited crowd outside. He let his black robe slip to the ground and, with an exhausted sigh, threw his wig at the door.

Translated by John Gallienne

IV
SIXTEEN POEMS

Yves Bonnefoy

Translated by Elsie MacGregor

Photograph of Yves Bonnefoy

Yves Bonnefoy was born on 24 June 1923 in Tours, studied mathematics, poetry and philosophy and published his first book in 1953. Aside from his reputation as one of the leading French poets of the present time, he has translated Shakespeare into French, won important literary prizes, and taught literature and poetry in France and the United States. Speaking of his own work he has said that for him "poetry is first of all a never-ending battle, a theatre where being and essence, form and formlessness fight each other fiercely."

SIXTEEN POEMS

TWO BARKS FROM DANS LE LEURRE DU SEUIL

The pending storm, the tumbled bed,
The shutter palpitating in the heat,
and the blood in its fever, I awaken
The closed hand from its dream, the ankle
From a bark's ring
Tied to a jetty in the surf,
And now the eyes, and now the absent mouth
And all this sudden wakening in the summer night
To bear within the storm until it ends
– Wherever you are when obscure I take you,
The roar of this sea thus increased in us,
Stay indifferent, let me embrace
– Almost like God the blind –
Matter to the utmost of its emptiness in night.
Take me ardently, but distractedly,
So that I have nor face, nor name,
And being thus the thief I can give you more,
And the alien exile in you, in me,
Can also be a source. Yes, I agree
However, forgetting you, I am with you.
If you unclose my fingers
And form with my palms a cup
I shall drink close to your thirst.
Then let the water run all over our limbs,
Water which makes us to be, even not being.
Water which cuts across our arid bodies
Being this joy which glimmers in the distance.
Enigma or presentiment! Do you remember
How we went through those fields choked with stone
And suddenly came on the cistern and these two presences

In some other country? of the arid summer?
See as they bend, do they, like ourselves,
Listen to us – of whom they speak,
Smiling under the foliage of the first tree
In their happy radiance, a little veiled?
And, should we not say, another ray of light
Moves in this harmony of their countenances
And, laughing, merges with them? See, the water moves
But the forms are purer, consumed.
Which is the real of these two worlds? No matter.
Invent me, enlarge me perhaps
On these confines of destroyed fable.
I listen, I consent,
Then I fling off the arm across my eyes
Disclosing to me the luminous face.
I touch the mouth with my lips,
In disorder, broken, an encompassing sea.
As God at sunrise I am arched
Over this water where our resemblance flowers.
I murmur: This, then, is what you want,
An unsatisfied power wandering among universes,
To be gathered up, a life, in the vase
Of the bare earth of our identity?
And it is true one instant all is silence,
It would seem time was coming to a halt
As if it hesitated on the way
Looking over the earthly shoulder
At what we cannot or do not wish to see.
Thunder no longer rolls in the calm sky,
The shower no longer falls upon our roof,
The shutter which rattled in our dream
Is silent, curved on its soul of iron.
I listen, not knowing to what sound, then rise
And search, still in the shadow, where I find
Last evening's glass half full.
I take it up; it gives back our breath,
I make you touch it with your obscure thirst,
And when I drink the tepid water touched by your lips
It is as if time ceased on mine
And that my eyes are open to the day at last.
. . . .

Peace on the lighted water. It seems that
A boat laden with fruit goes by;
And that a wave adequate and immobile
Overwhelms our reason, and this life
Like a boat, hardly different, is still moored.
Have confidence, and let yourself be borne, bare shoulder,
By the wave, enlarged through endless summer;
Sleep, it is high summer; and a night
Brilliant with starlight; begin to destroy
Our eternal night; smilingly
The Egyptian Queen bends over us.
Peace on the flowing wave. Time scintillates.
It seems the boat is motionless.
No longer do we hear the vast water
Hurl and disintegrate itself against the empty flank.

. . . .

I have entered
Into another universe.
It was before the dawn.
I threw salt on the snow.

DOUVE SPEAKS

1

Sometimes you said, wandering in the dawn
On darkened pathways
I shared the hypnosis of stone
Like it I was blind.
Now this wind has come by which my comedies
Are elucidated in the act of dying.

2

I yearned for summer
A furious summer which would dry my tears,
Now this cold has come, growing in my limbs,
I was awakened and suffered.

O fatal season,
O earth most bare as a blade,

I yearned for summer,
Who has broken the iron in the ancient blood?

Truly I was happy
Up to the point of death,
The eyes lost, my hand open to the soiling
Of perpetual rain.

I shrieked. I battled with my face against the wind.
Why hate, why weep, I was alive,
The deep summer, the day, reassured me.

3

Let the word die out
On this side of being where we are laid bare
Over this aridity crossed only
By the wind of finite things.

Let him who burned standing up
High as a vine,
Let the extreme singer roll from the crest
Illuminating
The vast incommunicable matter.

Let the word die out
In this low room where you rejoin me
Let the hearth of the cry be sealed
On the embers of our words,
Let the cold arise through my death and take a meaning.

VERITÉ

Thus until death, reunited faces,
The heart's awkward gestures over the body,
And on which you die, absolute truth,
This body abandoned in your enfeebled hands.

The blood's odour will be this good you sought,
Light of a single good over the orangery.
The sun will turn: its live agony
Lighting the place where all was unveiled.

VRAE LIEU

Let a place be laid for him who draws nigh
One who is cold and has no lodging.

One tempted by the rumour of a lamp
On the lit threshold of a single house.

And if he stays worn out with weariness
Let us recite for him the healing words.

What does this heart need where was but silence
If not words which are the sign and speech.

And like a sudden light seen in the night
And table half glimpsed in a poor dwelling.

PLACE OF THE SALAMANDER

The salamander, startled, is motionless
And feigns death.
Such is the first step of consciousness among stones
The perfect myth
A great fire crossed which is spirit.

The salamander was half way up the wall.
In the light from our windows
His glance was but a stone
But I saw his heart beat eternally.

O my accomplice and thought, allegory
Of all that is pure.
How I love him who encloses in his silence
The single force of joy.

How I love one who stays in harmony with the stars by the
        inert
Mass of his whole body.
How I love one who awaits the hour of his victory
And who holds his breath while clinging to the earth.

MENACES DU TEMOIN

The wind is still, lord of the oldest plaint,
Will I be the last one who takes arms for the dead?
Already the fire is but memory and ashes
Murmur of the closed wing, rumour of dead face.

Do you consent to love only iron of grey water
When the angel of your night shall come to close the port,
When he will lose in the motionless harbour water
The last gleams in the dead imprisoned wing.

Oh, submit only to my hard words,
And for you I will conquer sleep and death,
For you I will call up from the blighted tree
The flame which will be the boat and harbour.

For you I will raise up fire without time or place,
Wind seeking fire, summits of the dead wood,
The horizon of a voice where stars are falling,
And the moon merging with the dead's disorder.

LE BRUIT DES VOIX

Hushed were the murmuring voices naming you
Alone above the serried jostling boats.
Walk on this moving ground, but you keep
Another song than this grey water in your heart.

Another hope than this prepared departure,
These gloomy steps, this wavering light on the prow.
You do not like the stream whose waters are but terrestrial
And this moonlit pathway where the wind is still.

Rather, you say, rather on banks more dead,
The lofty ruin of the palaces that I was.
You love only night as night, which carries
The torch, your destiny, of all renouncement.

IN SAN FRANCESCO, EVENING

… So the floor was of marble in the dark room
Where incurable hope had brought you.
It seemed as though calm water with reflected lights
Carried far off voices of night and candles.

And yet no vessel asked for refuge there,
Nothing troubled the calmness of the water,
So I say to you, so are our other mirages
These festivals in our hearts, these enduring torches.

THE FINE SUMMER

Fire haunted our days and fulfilled them,
Its iron wounded time at each greyer dawn.
The wind howled death on the roof of our room.
Cold did not cease to surround our hearts.

It was a lovely summer, gusty and sombre,
You loved the gentleness of summer rain.
And you loved death which overhung the summer
With this trembling flag, its ashy wings.

That year you almost came to distinguish
A sign, black always, before your eyes,
Carried by stone, wind, water, leaves,

Just as the ploughshare cut into the newly turned earth.
And your pride loved this new light
The ecstasy of fear on the summer earth.

POVERTY

You will know he holds you in the dying hearth,
You will know he speaks to you, and stirring
The ashes of your body in the cold dawn
You will know he is alone and not yet comforted.

He who has destroyed so much; who no more knows

How to distinguish his emptiness from his silence,
He sees you, harsh dawn, from darkness come
And burn a long time on the waste of tables.

THE IRON BRIDGE

Doubtless there is still at the end of a long street
Where I walked as a child, a pool of oil,
A rectangle of weighty death under a black sky.

Since poetry
Has separated her waters from other waters,
Neither beauty nor colour retain her,
She is anguished for fire and night.

She nourishes
A long chagrin of dead shore, an iron bridge
Thrown across to the other shore still more nocturnal
Is her one memory and her one true love.

BEAUTY

She who ruins being, Beauty,
Shall be chastised, bound to the wheel,
Dishonoured, found guilty, made to let blood,
And cry, and night of all joy dispossessed,
O, torn on every gate before the dawn,
O stamped on every road and crossing.
Our high despair will be that you still live,
Our heart that you may suffer, our voice
To humiliate you in your tears, to call
You liar, purveyor of black sky.
Our desire still being your infirm body,
Our pity this heart leading to all mire.

IMPERFECTION IS THE SUMMIT

That was the truth; we had to destroy and destroy.
Sanity was only won at this price.

To ruin the naked face rising in the marble
Destroy all form, all beauty.

To love perfection because it is the threshold
But to deny it as soon as known, forget it dead.

Imperfection is the summit.

VENERANDA

He arrives. It is the gesture of a statue.
He speaks. His empire is among the dead.
He is a giant, he partakes of stone
Itself the sky of the dead's anger.

He grips. He lifts and holds above his face
Lamp which will burn in the country of the dead.
He protects from anguish and from death
The humble weeping body of the one who prays.

VENERANDA

He departs from her, he is another world.
Nothing will re-unite these foreign globes,
Not even this fire which in the hearth imitates
The greater fire that shines on empty worlds.

It is of small account that man went through
The stone and broke the ancient chains.
Long was this night. And many years
Have turned over the dark garden of the seas.

ON THE VOICE OF KATHLEEN FERRIER

All tenderness, all irony, were gathering here
For a farewell of crystal and of mist.
The deep metallic notes subdued to silence,
The brightness of the blade was veiled.

I sing the voice merged with grey tone that verges
On the far reaches of a vanished song
As if beyond all pure form there trembled
Another song, the one, the absolute.

O light and absence of the light, O tears
Smiling above all anguish and all hope.
O swan, true centre in the false dark water,
O dayspring when it was late evening.

It seems that you have knowledge of both shores,
The deepest grief, supremest ecstasy.
Down there among the grey weeds in the light
It seems you have a source of eternity.

V
TWENTY-FIVE POEMS

B.C. Leale

Photograph of B.C. Leale by Mark Gerson

B.C. Leale's first poem to appear in print was published in *The Observer* in 1961 and since then others have appeared in the *T.L.S.*, *Tribune*, *Poetry & Audience*, *Ambit*, *Stand*, *Slow Dancer* and *The New York Times* amongst other British and American periodicals. His work has also appeared in several anthologies including *A Group Anthology* (Oxford University Press). Other selections and single poem broadsheets available from small press publishers are *Under a Glass Sky*, *Boarding House* and *Preludes* (all three from Caligula Books), *Woman Alone* and *Loaves* (both Mandeville Press) and *Fouquet's* (Sceptre Press). B.C. Leale was born in 1930, educated at the Municipal College, Southend, and lives in London. His literary associations began with the latter days of 'the Group' and he is one of the few British poets to have absorbed and developed the influences of Dada and Surrealism. An earlier selection of his poems published in NWW 16 was highly praised by Peter Porter in *The Observer*.

TWENTY-FIVE POEMS

LEVIATHAN

White deafener unraveller of the thick-webbed deep
dazzling lit cathedral rising in a crater of spray
we feel the great lurch of your bones beneath us
your irredeemable dark chanting sounding within us

holy oil burning on the rim of night
baleful eye we would banish
down a forgotten watery hatchway
a cachalot engraved on paper

swallower of bodies wallowing
in the mire of mirrors flatteringly placed
the terrible silences of your eye
we go crouching out of

flailing white foundry rounding
on earth's emptiness
ivory nail scarring
the dark slate of the eternal.

THE VISIT

At the top
of the polished stairs where
the ambassador squeaks by

with his retinue
of stick-insects
blowing their
fine-boned noses

this woman
out of Bruegel
clutching a fish

sucks its head
and rolls about
grunting and sweating
on lurching earth.

IDEAL HOMES

The owners are out – you wouldn't know
they even existed, there are no
broken shoes lying about
or cushions oozing with stuff.

It helps somewhat to suddenly
shout, but it won't rock the monotonous hum
of the dust extractor, or foul the air
that's always fresher than fresh.

Even the goldfish have their fins
to their bodies locked, and float
like brooches pinned
to immaculate water.

LOAVES

How slowly they are brought out
wrapped in a hot
spicy steam

a careless finger
could disfigure their
piping sides

crusts nutty-flavoured
hot-buttered
honeyed

those distant days
sliding down ricks
of glossy cornstalks

climbing ladders
to yeasty heights
of cloudless nowheres

loaves baked to the rich
dark colour of
contentment.

CASPER GUTMAN (SYDNEY GREENSTREET) SPEAKS

Well, sir, you are, polishing the air with your cuffs,
enthroning your fist on a thick jaw,
quite a card,

a man very much, sir, after my own heart,
relishing a lingua fracas
in a room embellished with gunsmoke

– but to the point, sir, eschewing
these verbal dervishes
& fanfaronades: the bird, the falcon,

is jacketed in black, a black
plumage of paint, sir, a funereal armature over
an entassment of gold,

& worth ... ah, aha, h'm ... a cool
quarter million, a piece of feracious cake, sir,
for you too to partake of, a man of such furious nerve.

LOST WORLDS

Hotels Royal, Imperial, Grand –
stranded leviathans drying out
at the city's dead centre.

Furs, confections of feathers,
so gracefully taken,
jammed on hooks.

Slices of Battenburg, fragrant teas,
duchesses silvering the afternoons
with their polished venom.

Glissades of Gershwin
scarcely penetrating
walls slimed and cracked,

silent punch-ups
beneath iron grilles,
bodies kicked black.

SALON

Cigarillos cast espaliers of smoke
studded with jewels of aromatic wit.
Legs weak and tedious spindle down
and snake away from pontil marks on pools
full of loquacious grape.
Legs treadle into a cinereous dawn.

POSTCARD FROM MAURITIUS
(For Charles Thorne)

Gris-Gris (Souillac) enchants us by dashing against the
rocks Robert Edward Hart, the national poet. Not far away
are found wonderful spectacles in a charmed case of waves
breaking over "La Nef".

OFFER
(For Bernard J. Kelly)

Grand Metropolitan Hotels offer one-night concatenations.

Tears are inclusive of surreal rail travail but dada will be adad. English breakfast consists of two prunes of withered fur, a fresh cup of boiling unstirred fur and the tenderest bicycle wheels scrambled on toast. Reduced tears for a child if accompanied by an adult head chopped off or a wise saw.

WHERE IS YOUR HEADACHE?

– in a box of steam-hammers
– in a Ming vase filled with wine

– at the foot of an abyss
  built by Doré
– in the Fabergé egg where a motorcycle
  goes off in a roar of gold

IMAGINARY LANDSCAPE

between stations
squabbling birds
caged in the radio set

OUTSIDE MY GRANDFATHER'S FLAT

the stairs were dilapidated as music
profound holes around which
the entire orchestra sat
in concentrations of silence

& the postman ascended
brushing through
withheld glissandi of diamonds
clutching a long slippery envelope constructed of bones
aimed at someone's throat

LEARNING THE LANGUAGE

my snake has the measles
my little cousin sloughs his skin

the submarine dived and disappeared from its clothes
the gulls were dripping beneath the waves

my fishknife travels by sea
my fishwife is of chaste silver

your wife is hot air
your teacup is filled with invectives

the door smiled suddenly
the hinges fell out of her mind

she had lovely taste
she had aunts carved into furniture

BRIDEGROOM

he sat at the table
leaning upon the ocean

with a blade of marram grass
he slit his own throat
& lapped up the radiant blood

a tree screamed into the blackness

the wedding guests drifted
beneath carpets of kelp

the mourners took up the thousand and one positions
of sexual intercourse

POEM

greenflies trickle through air emeralds rain incessantly
on the grave of Carl Fabergé
a coal splits open a fern unfolds its bronze
rubescent with rubies

the Czar shakes ivory dice
splattered with black
gold typewriters soar from crags with talons clattering
    "murder"
bellowing elephants lift padded tusks
in resonant silence
moonlight is drenched with sonatas

AT THE CABARET VOLTAIRE, ZURICH (1916)

The room is dancing with nervous frayed
toothbrushes
the piano is packed with cordite and missionary zeal.

Hiccups are cut with scissors after a heavy dew
and vulgar fractions watered and autographed
in limited editions.

Tristan Tzara announces that mathematics
is a bubbling of mushrooms from the ribs of the Eiffel
    Tower
and that art is a blowlamp in the grip of a pig's trotters.

THE CONTENTS OF A VIOLIN CASE

Rocks. Feathers.
First carbon drafts of flight.
Hydrofoils planing an ocean.
Crystal clocks.

A billiard table's
liquid ivory. Tower blocks
soaked in flamingo
erased by night. Light-
ning's discharged crumpled gold.

FRACTURED LANDSCAPES

Teeth are in the viewfinder
the photographer's head is under a black cloth
the black cloth bursts in flames to reveal
a fish in a dark wood.

The viewfinder is under a lake
the lake is under a mountain
of teeth & exploding fish
in the photographer's ruined head.

FOR SALE & WANTED

A flock of tweezers adrift on the Sargasso Sea.
Thoughts emanating from the wood of a completely
    destroyed table.
The *Dreadnought* stuck between icebergs on Lake Chad.
A naked redhead at gale force 10 increasing.

WHAT MORE?

What more do you want
with your rooms full of chinoiserie
& the maids polishing steaming cases
of horse manure?

MUSEUM

You have stepped out of the museum
with its butterflies sawn in half
& its blonde chrysalids that spring up
quite unscathed.

There were photographs of yourself
in a cabinet of curiosities
& in states of anxiety Latin names

breathing out of the wall.

You have left the museum with its violent
thunderstorms stored in vaults
& its blinds drawn over the fading
colours of ancient dreams.

USEFUL OBJECTS TO HAVE ABOUT THE HOUSE

Pandemonium.
Green teeth.
A ship's mast.

An elephant brush.
Piano legs.
A jocular vein.

A stiff upper lip.
An ebullient boot.
Hairy eggs.

A pouncet-box.
A box on the ears.
An imperial sausage.

HAS ANYONE FOUND MY SIESTA?

Is it under the afternoon
        or a little
        to the side
full of oranges
full of diamonds
        on the hilts of daggers
weighed down by minute
        typography
        & abandoned hangars
full of dust
full of the rusting bones
        of disused trains

full of a piano concerto
    an elephant
    is extracting his teeth from?

OTHER WORLDS

The piano
feathers down
upon a city asleep

the dreamers
are leaving caves
of velutinous fire

& float over ivory roads
flanked by the black-
lacquered ilexes.

THE BIRD

Artillery
on both sides
bombarding the cage

howitzers
& 75s
a swish &

crump
as shells chip off
little bits of

rusted wire
& rattle
a heap of seed

but the bird
sits in black
acrid puffs

confident
his own voice
shaping a tune.

VI
BLOWOUT

Calum Ross

Photograph of Calum Ross with daughter

Calum Ross was born near Fort William, Inverness-shire, in 1946. He was brought up there and in Skye. He studied Art in the Glasgow School of Art in the sixties since when he has worked in various jobs. He now lives in Newton Stewart, Wigtownshire where he teaches Art, is married with two children and is currently working on a novel. This is his first published piece – the climax and ending of his first unpublished novel.

'Ahah,' he s
sleepin' there
At this,
been pro
forwa
unsu
sn

He looked around him. Big
in the armchair by the fire
glazed look to Crosby's
conversation.

'But John,' said Big Hughie, his iniineffectual pointing movements as he vainly tried to
interrupt Crosby's harangue, –

'John, I was, uh –'

'But why did he though?' continued the heedless Crosby,
blustering on regardless of the faltering Langholm, – 'Why
did he though, – eh?'

Big Hughie lurched forward in the chair. His eyes were
beginning to close.

He shifted his gaze from Langholm and Crosby and
discovered, slumped on the couch beside him, an almost
unconscious Sam MacLeod. Slavers trickled unheeded
from the slack corner of his gaping mouth, the lips of which
had a distinct and bloody puffiness to them, and his
laboured breathing seemed to begin somewhere in his
stomach.

'Eh?' MacLeod said, 'Eh?' But he was speaking to
nobody there: he was merely using the word as a device to
stay awake and the brevity of its syllable assured him only
an equivalent minimum of awareness.

On the floor at their feet were empty lager cans and
empty bottles and crushed carrier bags and fallen-over
glasses and the air in the room was so stuffed with stale,
still, cigarette smoke that it looked like a blue-grey gas. He
shook the sleep from his eyes and shivered.

'Who's got a fag?' he asked. 'Anyone got a fag?'

Big Hughie, still trapped in glazed audience, fumbled
robot-like in the deep pockets of his overcoat and without
any apparent awareness of his actions, handed over a
packet of cigarettes to him. Crosby stopped in mid sentence
at this and stared at MacPhail.

aid. 'You're awake are you? You've been
for bloody hours.'

ig Hughie, as if he had, all the while until then,
pped up on Crosby's stream of words, pitched
off his chair at their cessation and after a couple of
ccessful attempts at rising, became still and lay there,
uffling, his mouth wide open and his eyes tight closed.

MacPhail lit his cigarette and looked down at him.

'There's Hughie away,' he said.

'Aye,' Crosby replied, 'Bastard's always flakin' out. How
you feelin' yourself now Billy, – OK?'

'I'm feelin' hellish.'

'You've been sleepin' for hours an' bloody hours. Hughie
was sayin' you were like Rip van fuckin' Winkle.' He
laughed hoarsely at this with far more glee than the remark
deserved, and looked down blearily at the collapsed
Langholm.

'Eh?' MacLeod enquired. 'Eh?' Crosby failed to notice.

'Anyway,' he said, abandoning his laugh, 'Time for
another wee dram Billy, eh? – look, –' And he picked up a
bottle from beside his chair.

'Still some here. Come on, – it's the New Year.'

MacPhail began to reach out. Crosby knew what had
happened. He was doing this to taunt him. He hesitated.

'Ach,' he said, 'Maybe I'll no –'

'Ach nothin', – come on, – gerrit down your throat.'

'Ach, John,'

'Look, – there's plenty,' Crosby said, presenting his
provocation as generosity. 'You're welcome to it.' He held
out the bottle to him. 'It's whisky,' he said. 'Your old
favourite. What's stoppin' you MacPhail?' He leaned
forward. 'You thinkin' of givin' it up or somethin'?'

MacPhail flung his cigarette in the fire.

'You're no exactly against it yourself, Crosby.'

'Maybe I'm not,' Crosby said steadily, pronouncing his
words with exaggerated, showy care, 'But I think the likes
of yourself enjoys it far more than the likes of me.'

'Aye? You do, do you?' The cigarette had burned
brightly in the fire; only the ashes were left.

Crosby leered. 'Hey, look, Sam,' he called loudly to
MacLeod. 'MacPhail's awake an' he's shoutin' for more
drink.'

'Goo dole Billy MuPhail ...' mumbled MacLeod from far away on the brink of sleep.

MacPhail looked back at Crosby. He knew he was needling him. People did that. They looked for someone worse than themselves. It solaced them. Crosby was like that. But what did it matter? It was too late now for 'No.'

'Give me the bottle then Crosby, if it'll shut you up.'

'Oho, would you listen to the man,' said Crosby, and MacPhail took it from his hand and downed a great mouthful.

'You orright there Billy orright eh orright mmh?' MacLeod asked in a sudden rushing spate of slurred speech which did not alter his pose or flicker his eyes one whit.

'Yeh,' he said, 'Terrific.'

'What about yourself there, Sam,' Crosby asked. 'In the bloody horrors are you?'

'Eh? Mmmh? Mmmh?'

'Let the team down badly the night, didn't you?'

'Eh, eh?'

'He hears bloody fine,' Crosby said.

'How'd he let the team down?' MacPhail asked.

'You no' remember? Look at his mouth. He's no'goin' to forget about it.'

'What happened?'

'Over in the MacRae's house. Got us all put out.'

'How?'

'His usual carry-on. Girl's father caught him at it. Didn't he Sam?'

'Sharraap.' His eyes were beginning to open. 'Shahrrup.'

'Her old man burst down the lavvy door. They were in the bath the pair of them. Girl was plastered,–she's only a young thing. He was up to his usual. "Ya bastard" her old man says "Who d'you think y'are, – Errol Flynn?" An' he belted him right in the teeth. Then we all got kicked out. You no' remember?'

'Nuh'

'No wonder his wife buggered off.' Crosby said.

'Ehh? Mmh?'

'I said you're a dirty bastard MacLeod. I've got to work with that man.'

'Am I never to hear the end of it?' gagged MacLeod and he keeled over onto his side and became suddenly and uncontrollably sick.

'Get a basin, you pig, MacLeod!' shouted Crosby, whose home it was. 'Go on, – outside, – get the hell you bastard! Look at the couch for Christ's sake, – look at the mess you're makin'.'

'Come on, Sam' MacPhail said desperately. 'Don't be sick on the couch. Come on, come on, – get up.' And he began to slap his face.

'I'm orright. I'm orright.'

Crosby hauled him to his feet, his teeth clenched in rage.

'Why don't you spew outside, – you could've said you were goin' ta spew!'

'Sohhy John, sohhy John'

'Bastard! Well, come on Billy – gimme a hand to get him out before he lets the lot go!'

'I think he already has,' MacPhail said.

He climbed unsteadily to his feet, and then, slipping on the sickness splattered on the linoleum, he grabbed frantically at Crosby for support, but lost his balance and brought all three crashing in a heap to the floor, where MacLeod immediately became sick again, vile bile bursting forth in a gush from his puffy lips.

'For fuck's sake, it's in my hair,' screamed Crosby.

'Can't help it,' MacLeod blurted and gulped. 'Can't helpit.'

The noise wakened Big Hughie and he tried to rise, but the small fireside rug skiddered from under his feet and he pitched sideways into the fire, knocking over a fireside companion with a crashing jangle of pokers and tongs. MacPhail jumped to his feet, and miraculously keeping his balance, pulled Langholm clear.

'Oh Christ, I'm burning!' screamed Langholm too late. 'I'm burning, I'm burning!'

'Get that daft cunt out of the fire!' Crosby yelled, slithering in panic on the lino.

'He's all right,' MacPhail said. 'You're all right Hughie,' and he placed him back in the fireside chair. His hair was singed but he was unmarked otherwise.

'A close shave ...' he began, but his words became mumbled and his eyes closed, and he went back to sleep, his mouth, as usual, agape.

Crosby had by this time slithered cursing to his feet, his

jacket smothered horribly with vomit.

'You pig MacLeod!' he screamed in blind rage, 'You dirty fucking pig!' And he began to kick the whimpering MacLeod but after one or two flaccid, ineffectual blows, he again stumbled on the slippery linoleum and fell backwards on top of a small low table which immediately parted into two with a flat cracking sound.

MacPhail swayed unsteadily on his feet and felt suddenly nauseous. The dingy room, the acrid, sickly smell, the squalor, the scrabbling amongst vomit, the bare bulb shining bitterly down, its brightness piercing like a fang.

'Look,' he said, 'Why –'

'Shut your fuckin' mouth, MacPhail,' said the seething Crosby, 'And help me up from here, – he's got it comin' to him!'

'Christ, has there no' been enough damage for one night, – look at the mess!'

'I'm sorry I'm sorry,' MacLeod slobbered pathetically.

'Sorry?' Crosby told him as he slithered closer in the slime on the floor, 'I'll bloody sorry you, ya baga shit!'

'Shurrup, the pair of you, – you'll waken the whole house!' MacPhail cried, but the door was thrown open then and Crosby's wife barged in, furious in her nightgown.

'Oh my God!' she shrieked. 'John Crosby you've shamed us all!'

Sam MacLeod, who until then seemed to have been recovering his faculties by the minute, immediately relapsed upon hearing her voice. Crosby's wife stared fiercely at the damage and mess in the room and then her eyes alighted on MacLeod and they narrowed with real venom.

'Sam MacLeod,' she said, the rage in her voice condensing in to a piercing hiss. 'What brings the likes of you into my house?'

'It's my house an' all,' put in Crosby without much enthusiasm.

'Shut up you bloody pig.'

'Christ's sake, Joanny' Crosby muttered.

'Well he's got a bloody nerve,' she burst out, 'Comin' to this house after what happened last New Year. Nobody can do that sort of thing to me, – or any woman – and expect it to be forgotten, – I don't care!'

"His usual carry-on," MacPhail remembered Crosby's phrase. The sickly Sam seemed a man of unfortunately regular habits.

'Mmh?' Langholm enquired drowsily. Johnny's voice had got to him but it seemed not to have reached MacLeod. He did not speak or move, nor did he show any sign of being capable of either. He lay where he had chosen to remain, settled in his own sickness.

'And now look at this stinking mess,' Joanny cried out, 'I'm sick of all this drunkenness, – sick of it!'

'It was MacLeod,' Crosby told her.

'And what were you doin' to stop it?'

'I –'

'Don't interrupt me,' she screeched at him 'I don't want your bloody lies, – I've been hearin' them for years – Oh my God!' she cried and leapt back, clutching her nightie about her legs.

MacLeod had furtively opened one eye and she had caught him peering lewdly and blearily up her bare legs. On being discovered by the outraged Joanny Crosby, he hastily and guiltily closed the eye and tried to pretend that he had been sleeping all the time. He then ruined this ruse by opening the other eye to see if anyone was taking the point. In spite of everything, MacPhail grinned.

'Oh John Crosby, see if you don't get these animals out of here I'll get the Police – I will, – I'm not kidding!'

'Aw bloody hell Joanny, – it's the New Year isn't it?'

'New Year – New Year! – God if I'm not sick of the New Year, – it was New Year three whole days ago!' Her rage soared to a new height.

'Get out of this house the lot of you,' she screamed. 'Go on, – get out right now!'

In the stunned silence which invariably follows such outbursts, they realized for the first time that the children in the upstairs room were crying. It was at this point also that Big Hughie surprised everyone by climbing unaided to his feet and saying through his slurs and mumbles,

'Quite right Joanny, Joanny's quite right, come on boys, – play the game.'

She seemed taken aback by this unexpected understanding but determined that her rage be not thwarted by goodness, she turned on MacPhail and directed it at him.

'And what are you doing here, Billy MacPhail, – you that's been off the drink for years? Did you not have enough of it? You should be blooming well ashamed of yourself, – you'll be sorry for this carry-on yet, just you wait and see.' And she burst into tears then and ran up the stairs to where the children were crying and crying.

'Joanny's right,' he thought, 'I will feel sorry,' but he tried to think of other things, for he knew that if he were to think of what had happened it would unleash an avalanche of remorse. He pulled up his coat collar against the cold and kept walking.

'Hey, Billy.' Big Hugh stumbled along beside him on the dark road his repetitive mumblings withering into wordless heavy breathing which, after a moment or two, would burst out again, jarring and insistent. 'Hey Billy, listen, listen.'

"What?"

'Hey Billy, look, listen, I'm sorry about the boys putting you off the tack and that.'

'Auch, the hell with it now, it's done isn't it.'

'No it's no Billy, no it's no, no it's no.'

McPhail was still drunk, but it was not the indifferent drunkenness of Langholm, it was a black drunkenness which lent energy to his sense of failure and self resentment and it could easily become directed angrily upon Langholm with his stupid, endless repetition. Langholm stopped and stood there swaying in the dark.

'Tell me this now Billy, tell me this, how long were you on the tack so to speak – off the drink like, how long was it like – eh, how long Billy, how long and that?'

'Three years.'

Three years – whoo – that's a long time Billy isn't it? that's a hell of a long time, it is you know. Do you know this Billy do you know this, I don't think you should ever start again – I mean that, don't ever do it again, don't it's not worth it. No it's not.'

McPhail's anger against himself seethed up in him with a great heat. 'You don't have to tell me that, you don't have to tell me that, I know. Jeez if I had a gun I would fucking shoot myself – I would. Do you know this, three years I've been down south – three miserable, bastarding years, living on my own, coming straight home from work every night and closing the door – never going out in case I would meet someone and start again, living like a hermit, avoiding people. Do you know what I used to do at nights? – jig-saws!'

'Jiggy-jig?'

'Jigsaw puzzles you bastard Langholm – fucking jig-saw puzzles every night, that's what I used to do for years, jig-saws puzzles. Of boats and trains and Christ knows what all. Houses and pictures of scenes for ages, and then I used to think I was starting to get it under control and I'd say yes I'm getting it, it's coming, I can do it, I know I can, I'm OK. And I was sure of it, I was sure of it for years and I come back up here saying it'll be OK it'll be OK and what happens? Bang. Three years pished up against the wall! I could shoot myself. I could shoot myself!'

'Auch it'll pass Billy. You'll get over it, you'll go back on the tack. You will.'

'Oh aye,' said McPhail bitterly, 'it's hell of an easy.'

'Oh I know it's not easy, I know it's not, but all the same there's a hell of a lot worse off in the world than you and me.'

'Oh aye,' McPhail agreed emptily, 'there's millions.'

'Ah there is though,' said Big Hughie, and he became silent and lurched along unsteadily, his shoes crunching in the gravel. McPhail kept an erratic pace with him; stooped in his crushed raincoat, he plagued himself with the bitter poisons of his self-disgust and dour remorse; his hands were fists thrust deep in his raincoat pockets, his arms were rigid and his eyes blazed with a lost past.

When Big Hugh fell he fell heavily; one could be forgiven for thinking that he must surely have broken something for a man of his size falls like a factory chimney. McPhail, smitten as he was with his own self castigation and rage, was not at that moment blessed with a sense of charity nor were his responses kind; instead, the collapse of his friend induced in him an explosion of unrestrained vilification.

'You bastard don't flake out on me,' he screamed, 'not here Langholm you drunken bastard – waken up will you, waken up instead of lying there pissed out of your mind. Waken up Langholm! d'you expect me to carry you home? I'm bloody sure I don't – not after what you did to me – you and your fucking mates Langholm – it was all your bloody fault you shower of cunts – you got me plastered after all these years!' He kicked savagely at the fallen Langholm. 'Shitehawks all of you,' he cried, 'bastards!' Maddened he seized Langholm by the lapels and tried to drag him to his feet; as he did so a half-bottle jutted up suddenly from inside Big Hugh's jacket, and this infuriated him further. 'You gutsy miserable bastard will you get up! – get up or I'll bloody kill you.' Langholm's head lolled floppily from side to side and he snored softly. Snatching up the half-bottle McPhail leaped to his feet and Langholm's head bumped lumpily off the road. 'All right then, have it your own way Langholm but I'm taking this – you can lie there, you can rot in hell – let the cars get you, lorries – I don't care you coniving bastard,' and still shouting he ran off into the dark clutching the half bottle.

When McPhail fell, his fall was not the deft, wordless, plumping exit from consciousness of Big Hugh Langholm, no, McPhail's was a harsh rasping scraping thing of raucous cursing amongst skidding gravel and breaking glass and one would not have been surprised were it to have produced a jet of sparks like a grinder's wheel.

He dragged himself aching to his feet and discovered his winded limbs amongst scraped knees, skinned palms and jolted shoulders; ahead of him on the road the half-bottle lay shattered in a thousand bits. He sat on the roadside verge and moaned; it had all gone wrong, it was all of it ruined for him and he suddenly grew afraid of his tomorrow – a tomorrow haunted by the dry ghosts of his failure – treatment, antabuse pills, nightmares; perhaps this time there was no chance, perhaps having now failed he had thrown away his chance and was stuck on it forever, like being on a roundabout which he would never be able to get off, stuck on a wooden horse going nowhere, going faster and faster, everyone hurrying and hurrying round and round and round – the image whirled in his mind in a blur and he turned over on the grass and was sick.

The night was mild and dark, clouds like soft masses of darkness parted and showed their most secret stars and white showers on the far hills: there was no bird sang for him there, there was no fruit that he might eat growing there in the forests of the night; only, in his mouth he tasted of the bitter fruits of his sickness and in his heart he tasted the bitter fruits of his failure. And that last bitterness seemed big enough to share with all the world.

Here was a jig-saw which he could never complete for it kept growing bigger and bigger and more and more of a puzzle; a year ago – a week ago, the situation in which he now found himself would have been unthinkable, impossible, a nightmare, but here he was and it was real. And yet. And yet deep down, he now realized, he had been prepared, expecting it always for this was nothing more than the crisis for which he had been preparing these past three years – The Big Blowout. Most of the past two or three days was lost on him, true there were blurred glimpses and flashes of brilliant clarity but most of it was lost and that was perhaps as well. He could remember Crosby's house and what had happened after waking but he could remember nothing of how he had come to be there – not that it mattered, for it was not what he had done whilst drunk that was so bad as the fact that he had got drunk in the first place. A dark gloom of self-rebuke descended upon him, stirring once again in his mind the image of the roundabout whirling and spinning, destroying him. He shook his head and looked around him seeing without much interest a car's headlights hurrying towards him through the night. And suddenly, as though cold water had been flung over him he remembered Langholm lying on the road. For a few uncertain moments he sat motionless, confused – had he not said to hell with Langholm, was all this not Langholm's fault anyway, all this misery of his, all this mess; he faltered, and then jumped to his feet and began running along the road.

'Wait,' he cried, 'wait, I'm coming, waken up Langholm, waken up – stop!'

The lights were closer now, their rays scything round corners in the dark, the wheels spinning closer and closer, to Langholm's head, closer to his curved spine, closer to his crushable skull with its intricate brain, injury, paralysis, death, murder – they were all in those wheels smashing closer and closer.

'Oh God!' he cried in sudden anguish 'I'm running the wrong way, – he's behind me – no, no!' He stopped, gasping for breath, 'Oh Jesus! Jesus Christ help him help him, please help him,' and madly, his lungs bursting, he

ran back the way he had come. The light from the car was
beginning to pick out details of the road before him, the
fences, the fields on either side, he could hear it more
clearly now, closer, closer, he began to choke – a stitch
burning in his side burned deeper and deeper and then he
was falling, falling amongst the gravel on the roadside.
'Langholm Langholm, – waken up Langholm.' His legs
were sapped of all their strength; they were like rubber,
shaking, quivering. The headlights were throwing his own
shadow now, flashing on the road before him, closer and
more swiftly closer, nearer, nearer – he would never reach
Langholm in time, not now, it was too late, burning tears
sprang to his eyes, Langholm was going to die, this was his
doing, his fault, his murder. And then he realized in a flash
that this wouldn't happen at all, he could stop the car, he'd
been running for nothing, no reason – the car was behind
him, he had only to wave it down to stop it. And then, just
when he'd realized this the lights turned away, up a lane off
the road and it was over and Hugh Langholm was safe.

He staggered onwards, his breath choking him, his heart
thudding thudding in his chest like a hammer, trembling
haltingly, shaking with effort on legs which he had barely
the strength to lift. Exhausted, he stumbled and fell heavily
over the outstretched legs of

'Hughie Langholm!'

And it was. Langholm the source of his worry and
exhaustion and woe, Langholm lying where he had left him
snoring in contentment, swaddled in the bliss of deep and
restful sleep.

'See you Hughie Langholm,' gasped McPhail hoarsely as
he lay back exhausted against Langholm's bulk, 'see you,
you bloody near killed me the night.' And he closed his eyes
and after a few moments he began to laugh in hoarse
painful gasps.

McPhail trudged along the dark road supporting, not
without difficulty, the snuffling step dragging hulk of
Hughie Langholm; were anyone to have seen them
stumbling under the light of the newly risen moon they
would have found little splendour in the appearance of
either, but Big Hugh was without doubt the most trampish
and tousled of the pair with his long scuffy overcoat muddy
and besmirched with filth and sickness, his hair splatched
across his chalky face and his eyelids hovering endlessly on

an eerie borderline between waking and sleeping. Barely pronounced words blotted plastering through frothy scum on his slack lips and sporadic hiccuping imploded resonantly in his chest; and yet McPhail carried him without complaint.

'You're all right Hughie,' he'd say, 'you're OK pal.'

McPhail the guilt ridden did these things, McPhail the penitent, making amends for his drunken robbery and near-murder of the hopeless, hapless, rag-bag, raggle taggle and now so very precious, Hughie. 'You're OK old friend, keep your chin up pal that's the stuff.' And so he went on prattling his inane words of encouragement that he might ingratiate himself with Langholm and by doing so, atone in some obscure way for what he had done. 'You're doing fine there Hughie – great.'

He saw the dark trees scrawled in twigs against the lightening sky and the grey panes of moonlit fields; now and then a house appeared, inching by across fields as they plodded past, and silvery moonlit scenes in the far distance were swallowed up in the darkness by overlays of cloud on the moon. The weight of his burdens bore heavily upon him and as they trudged onwards he held further court with his conscience and bitterly indicted himself on an ever-growing number of counts; further flickers of uncertain memory tormented him with shame and remorse, bringing back to him his fear of treatment which would not succeed. He set his mind to it suddenly, halting in mid step – there would be no more clinics and no more pills, he would do what had to be done and he would do it on his own; he would do it the hard way and succeed.

'God strike me down dead,' he cried, 'if I ever drink another drop again.' The bond was made, it was done, they proceeded.

As they journeyed on, the cold wind which had sprung up from the West freshened and the cool swashes blowing over them grew chill, the branches of the trees creaked coldly in the fields and Langholm, shivering, began to come round.

'Who's this,' he asked through his chattering teeth, casting blurred eyes on McPhail, 'who's this here – eh?'

'You're all right Hughie, you're OK my friend.'

'Billy McPhail! Oh here I feel hellish Billy. Jeez it's cold,

cold – where've we been anyway eh?'

'Crosby's.'

'Crosby's? Crosby's that's right – Crosby's – what's the time?'

'I don't know – can you walk a bit now?'

Langholm unslung himself from his helper and began to walk. 'I'm OK, I'm OK.' But he was staggering badly, his body weight seemed to leap heavily from right to left and he had to make swift plunging races to maintain it within the scope of his balance. McPhail seized hold of him by the shoulder: 'You're all right – we'll manage like this, together.'

'Good on you Bill.'

It had been McPhail's sense of guilt and retribution which had induced him to take Langholm all the long road to his home; he had only a vague idea as to where exactly on the road his house was for he had never really known Langholm well, and before this New Year, mostly by sight. God only knew why they should have landed together over the last couple of days.

Gradually the cold and the concentration of walking revived Langholm, restoring his awareness and his balance and clearing his breathing of its slurs and hics.

'How far is it now Hughie?'

'Not far, we're nearly there.'

'How you feeling now?'

'Oh, I feel hellish – I'm going to have to stop this boozing carry-on, it's just a bloody waste of time, no to mention money. It's a terrible thing when you think of it Billy, isn't it – the booze?'

'Aye.'

'I'm going to stop it – I am. See when this New Year's over – that's me, no more – finito.'

'I'm off it and all, I'm finished with it, that's it over now, Hughie, that's the last of it.'

'Quite right Billy, you're quite right, no more booze. Do you know this?' he added with a heavy sort of brightness, 'I'm feeling a lot better now. I was really pretty bad for a while there, I must have flaked out and all.'

'Auch you'll be all right by the time you get home. Where's your house anyway?'

'Look, do you see that light over there? – well that's it.'

'They're still up?' asked McPhail in surprise.

'Oh aye, the light's – well the light's always on.'

'It's no on all night long surely?'

'Aye.'

'Jeez, Langholm's Dirty-Dancer, Langholm's All-night Eater-Upper.'

Langholm said, 'Langholm's All-night Eater-Upper fuck-all,' and sensing something in the way it was said, McPhail left it at that.

As they neared the house, McPhail, on seeing that Langholm seemed sober and steady enough to take care of himself, told him that he would surely manage the rest of the way on his own and that he, McPhail, had better be getting home himself. Langholm then expressed his profound and sincere – and to McPhail acutely embarrassing – gratitude for the latter's 'kindly assistance'; it was apparently, 'far more than many a man would do' and 'not to be snuffed at.' He then insisted that his 'guardian angel' (his own words) should participate with him in the homely and stimulating ritual of 'a cup of tea and a half loaf'. McPhail protested and professed a stern reluctance which was totally at variance with his true feelings. 'It would,' he told the earnest Langholm, 'give me the boke.' Langholm however chose to ignore this remark and insisted upon his hospitality being accepted, indeed, he extended it even further by including within its terms 'a plate of soup that would put hairs on your chest.'

McPhail's obdurate intransigence was instantly overcome and he there and then gave verbal confirmation of his gastronomically induced tergiversation with the jubilant cry, 'Hullo the boat! a plate of soup – bloody lovely Hughie.' And they went towards the door.

Before they entered, Langholm turned to McPhail, and in a low voice said, 'Give us a loan of your comb will you.' McPhail was taken aback but nevertheless obliged and watched in surprise as his shabby, dishevelled companion combed his hair, straightened his coat, smoothed down the creases, rubbed off the dirt, blew his nose and buttoned himself up. 'How does that look – OK?'

'Bloody awful – you can keep the comb,' he added quickly, forestalling its return as he remembered the dubious pillows on which Langholm's head had rested during the course of the evening.

'Come on in then, Billy.'

McPhail found himself in the dimly lit kitchen of a croft house; the dark green paint on the wood walls was obviously old as was the faded sepia photograph in the skewed frame, the stopped pocket-watch hanging from a nail, the coronation mug, and the big, cracked willow-pattern plate perched precariously on a high shelf which looked like the last surviving member of an old, old, wedding present and, as is always the way, being last, the more vulnerable still. A cast iron range set in the far wall showed within its barred grate a birch block fire burning low; McPhail caught the sharp wooden smell at once, and saw the kettle stirring with a soft burr on the hob.

'Sit down Billy, don't be a stranger.'

'Nobody up?' he asked in a low voice.

'Auch aye, there's always somebody up.' He opened a cupboard and took out some cups. 'Our wee sister doesn't keep well, ach she's no been well for a while you know. There's usually one of us stays up with her.'

'Jeez I didn't know, Hughie, sorry to hear that.' Serious illness – he could tell that by Big Hughie's apologetic evasiveness. God Almighty, why had he come here – a stranger in this house of sadness?

'Here Hughie, I don't want to butt in like, maybe I better –'

'Ach don't be daft Billy, the tea's on and look, here's the soup.' He peered into the black pot. 'Just the job,' he told McPhail, 'lentil soup,' and he busied himself with the plates.

McPhail, sitting at the creaky table, sensed in the other man's fidgeting and busyness a process of deception, of distraction at work; the clack of a plate or the ring of a spoon on a cup; they all in their small, nervous ways told of some suppressed feeling in disguise.

'I'm sorry to hear things aren't so good, Hughie.'

'Ah well that's the way.' The door of the room opened unexpectedly and a woman came in; she was in her thirties, probably around Hughie's age, and as she gently closed the door she smiled at McPhail.

'Oh hullo,' he said and rising uncertainly to his feet, took her hand and wished her a Happy New Year. 'Happy New

Year,' she replied. But she said it as if it would all be his.

'Ah Billy, this is my sister Margaret. Do you mind of Billy McPhail Maggie?'

'Oh aye I think so; you're from Torlundy or somewhere like that aren't you? You've been away for a while.'

'Aye that's right.'

'We're making tea,' said Hughie. 'You wanting a cup? There's soup in the pot and all.'

She said she knew there was soup in the pot, it was lentil soup and she had made it, and sit down she would get it ready, and where had he been all night anyway?

'Ach we landed over at Crosby's.'

'Was there many there?'

'Ach the usual crowd; was there anybody here?'

'No, no one;' she turned to McPhail. 'You're our first foot.'

'Jeez and I don't have anything with me.'

'Here comes your soup,' said Hughie, 'By Christ, – Billy this'll stick to your ribs.'

'Mind your language you,' said Maggie.

'Lovely,' said McPhail. And they all sat down to eat at two in the morning.

Dong dong went the soft gong of the wag-at-the-wa'gone two; the fat old cat in the armchair at the fireside stirred briefly, looked round and yawned and then went back to sleep buffered from the poky springs of the burst chair by shock-absorbing newspapers. The calendar for the year that had gone hung still on the wall by the range unnoticed; December 31st, – the last recorded message from the parted year; by the grate a pair of boots, on the mantlepiece a dark bottle of pills. And clack went the clock and click.

'Are the old folks in bed Maggie?'

'Aye.'

'How's Bella been?'

'Oh she wasn't bad the day. She heard you coming in. "There's our first foot," she says. "First foot my foot," I says, "It'll be Hughie knocking things over." But she was right. You'll have to go up and see her Billy, she's wide awake – she sleeps off and on you see.'

'Oh aye,' said Hughie in a voice full of appeal and excitement, 'Go up first footing her, she'd love that – look

I'll tell you what, we'll all go up thegether – hold on and I'll get the booze.'

As they climbed the stairs McPhail was smitten by a feeling of being trapped; events had moved not so much quickly as unexpectedly, and left him in a position which he himself would not have sought. He wished somewhere in his heart that he could turn and say Goodnight and leave the house, that he could put it all aside and choose alone the going out and the coming in; but no, before him up those stairs was a sickly girl to whom events dictated he should bring good wishes with a cheerfulness he could not feel, and there on these steps before him climbed the dark bulk of Big Hughie Langholm, holding in one hand, like some improbable waiter, a shining tray of clinking glasses, and in the other a bottle of whisky.

The air in the room had that stuffy, breathed quality which bedrooms have when they have been slept in late into the day. McPhail discovered it immediately and noticed too the mingled, pale tang of disinfectant and air freshener all of which together blended into the universal sickroom air. A sparsely furnished room aloft in a night-time house, and in a loose and scattered bed, weakly rising, sick and thin was Langholm's sister.

'Hullo Bella,' said Big Hugh, 'Look who's here, your first foot of the year Billy McPhail – The Man Who Ate The Boiled Ham Raw.'

'Happy New Year Bella, how you feeling?'

'Happy New Year Billy.'

'You were right enough Bella,' said Maggie, 'It was your first foot after all.'

'Aye and I got the blame, didn't I Bella? – said it was me knocking things over – look –' Hughie rose on tiptoe and did a heavy Pas-de-Bas. 'Look who's light footed,' he said. 'Do you know what they call me at the dances?'

'Clod-hopper.'

'Aw come on, "Clod-hopper" what do you mean "Clod-hopper"?'

'Just what she says,' Maggie told him. 'Sarah McLean in The Village told me you took her up once and you damn near broke her leg.'

'Not at all,' said Hughie, winking at Bella, 'She must have stuck her foot down a hole in the floor.' Bella laughed

in a frail way and then asked, 'Where were you till now
Hughie? I thought you would have been back early.'

'Well it's only January yet isn't it? – you can't get much
earlier than that.'

They talked on in their curious bantering way; McPhail
watched the girl – she seemed only about sixteen, thin-
faced and wasted, her skinny arms outside the covers and
her big hollowed eyes alternately bright and dull. 'And
look,' said Langholm taking hold of McPhail's sleeve –
'Here's the very man who led me astray – the Very
Reverend Old Bagascrewtops himself – isn't that right
Billy?'

'Oh aye – I'm the world's worst.'

'See – he'll tell you himself. But now then Bella,'
continued Hughie, carefully arranging the glasses on the
tray and glancing at McPhail, 'Now then, did you get a
New Year dram yet?'

There was a feeling came upon McPhail then, a confused
resentful feeling, apprehension, a tiny faraway voice saying
'No', but he broke the seal on Hughie's bottle as pre-
arranged saying, 'Here's a wee New Year to you Bella, a
wee dram for luck.'

Liquid Gold – the stench of it struck his nostrils like fire,
herein lay the source of his disaster, his hands shook as he
held it. Three years famine from this hellfire-water had been
ended, three years of steady health and better days, three
years of winning lost and thrown away for nothing, nothing
but waste. His hands trembled in agitation, had he not said
tonight already that he was finished of it – had he not
promised, and having done that was he now to start again?
And again and again and again, back on the downward
career, back on the roundabout, back to the dosser days
and back to the clinic to confess the failure of his will – all
because of Langholm bringing him here to this house and
this room and this crossroads. What of that promise he had
– made on the journey home, – that terrible bond struck
before his God?

Langholm had begun to cast uneasy glances, sensing in
some vague way a conflict in McPhail, a suspicion that
something was going wrong.

Why was he here in this house of death? God had sent
him here to test the value of his word, to weigh his worth, to

try him out – how could he go back on that pledge? He felt
the heat rising into his head and heard, vaguely, the bottle
knocking amongst the glass on the tray. His eyes lighted
suddenly upon the girl, her eyes grown tired now were
turned upon him, dull with unadorned lacklustre
listlessness, disclosing mutely that she suffered there, no
matter how her pain be blunted down with drugs, she
suffered, young and dying on the brink of this Good Year. A
wave of pity stole from his heart and he felt crushed beneath
a mingled sense of shame, for there in her sick and
unaffected eyes he saw reflected plainly just how mean his
thoughts had been, how insignificant his selfish woes and
how great his wealth in having what he had compared to
her who had so little left. A sense of sadness which was
almost grief filled him for the dying girl and he felt some
deep-down, honest part of him protest against the cruel
waste of her young life. He stilled his hand and poured the
drinks; what God would grieve should he, in lifting up his
glass and wishing this poor girl good health, drink down
another drink and break his pledge?

'Here we are,' he said, distributing the glasses, 'here we
are and a Good New Year to one and all – Bella, your good
health.'

'A Good New Year to you Bella,' they said together, and
they lifted their glasses and Bella said, 'A Happy New Year
everyone,' and she touched the glass to her lips and smiled.

They came down the stairs in silence, the glass shivering
on the tray, the wood beneath them and in the walls
creaking as they descended, as though the house were
talking in its sleep. McPhail glanced slowly round him
wondering what lay behind each closed door – here perhaps
was their old mother and father, sleeping their wrinkled
sleep in the beds of old age, faltering through arthritic
dreams, stumbling against Time. Perhaps behind this door
was a cupboard full of old clothes and boots and shoes,
some of them Bella's, covered in dust, discarded, the
earliest details of her passing, the first visible, tiny, tip of
her death; those doors down there, cold empty rooms full of
darkness and silence, wardrobes with eerie, half-open doors
and shadows and people in photographs staring out of the
frames, peering into the dark. And upstairs, alone in the
stillness, Bella dying with the lights on. 'Our wee sister

doesn't keep well.' He shivered and longed to be gone.

When they were back in the kitchen he wished there was something he could say to them in their troubles, some words of sincere consolation which would convey the pity he felt but all he could find to say was that he was 'awful sorry about Bella' and he left it at that for he had no wish either to enlarge upon his ineffective words or pry further into the sadness of their affairs. Hughie poured out two massive whiskies, but McPhail would take no more and said he would have to be going. 'It's getting late,' he told them.

'Here, you're no walking to Torlundy, Billy?'

'Auch I'll try and get a taxi – is there a phone around anywhere?'

'You don't need a taxi – I'll take you over.'

'But the van's broken down, Hughie,' said Maggie.

'I know it is but I'll still get Billy home, don't you worry,' and he drank McPhail's whisky as well as his own and said, 'Come on then, Billy and I'll show you the alternative transport. He took him outside, round to the back of the house and there, in an old barn he proudly showed McPhail what he meant – an old motorcycle combination covered in dust and hen-droppings. 'This bike's been lying here for years Billy, I used to go everywhere on it – the old sidecar and all, it was great – but then I got the van and, auch, I never really bothered with it. Many's the time I thought I would sell it, but no, I always hung on to it – look at it Billy it's a beauty isn't it? – twenty years old and still good for the road. A bloody great bike, it really is. Anyway the van packed up a couple of weeks ago, it's needing a hell of a lot done to it – in fact I think it's knackered, so one night before the New Year I thought to myself, here, I think I'll go and have a look at the old bike, see what she's like, you know, and I started on it. Didn't need much at all, it didn't – just a bit fixed here and there and then chug chug chug – away she went, no bother. It's five years anyway since I had her on the road and look at her, she's going like a wee clock, aye,' he added nostalgically, 'they're great things the old motorbikes.'

McPhail looked at the dust on the windows of the sidecar and the corrosion on the mudguards and mountings; there were cobwebs and dead wasps in the spokes and there was mould on the seats and the tyres were bald. 'Aye, they were great things the old motorbikes,' he thought drily, 'very good in their day.'

'Are you sure I couldn't get a taxi Hughie – maybe I could –'

'Taxis bi Christ,' exploded Hughie, 'what in the hell do you mean taxis? – this is your taxi. Come on and give us a hand to get it out and we'll be started up and away in no time. Taxis! you and your taxis.' And McPhail, without giving further expression to his reluctance, grudgingly obliged. Langholm got the machine going without much difficulty, but the 'wee clock' aspect of its roars was hardly apparent to McPhail. Unlike Langholm he had no great love of motorbikes, instead what he felt for them was more of a fear than anything else and as he climbed uneasily into the rickety sidecar which stank decisively of cats and hens and sour oil, he had a sudden gut-tightening feeling of being trapped and sealed in a thin shell of metal and grimy perspex, where he felt vulnerable and afraid. He rubbed the dirt off the perspex and through the dim sweep left by his hand he saw Maggie waving to them from the open doorway as they moved off, the light shining behind her. He waved back, but the windows were so dirty she would never see, and then they were gone, roaring and shaking into the night.

McPhail had been drunk for days and during that time, despite the fact that he had consumed a vast quantity of drink, he had hardly eaten at all and what little sleep he'd had had been snatched fitfully on chairs and on floors; all this was beginning to tell on him and it was in his mind that he would pay the greatest price for his excess. McPhail had always in the past been prone to collossal depressions in the wake of drinking bouts; remorse far in excess of reason would beset him for long terrible days and he would suffer a mental despair which could only be described as anguish. Tiny incidents would flash with incredible power in his brain, incidents which, were he to consider them calmly with a cool detachment, would be seen as mere trivia, appeared to him in times like these to be episodes of grotesque importance, summoning up from the swarming darkness of his mind all sorts of involved chaotic trains of thought which were charged with profound anxiety and self-horror, tormenting him and causing him sometimes to groan and cry out aloud in his despairing pain against his deeds and against himself. Now as he sped away from Langholm's home on the rattling swaying sidecar, the uneasy fear he felt became exacerbated by the unsteady state of his nerves; his already tremulous hands shook all· the more and as his fears increased, so did his mind become nakedly vulnerable to irrational and vivid fears – dark pictures swelled up from his memory and overflowed into his agitated thoughts, infusing them with unreality.

He cleared the grime off the windscreen and looked out; Langholm was going too fast – he was going far too fast – why did he have to go at this speed, could he not slow down – take care? The verges swept past and the bushes and trees and the road rushed out of the night and whizzed below him; into his mind flashed a sudden picture of himself in his precarious seat, hurtling through the air, mere inches from the stones on the road, these hard sharp stones that could rip through his soft warm flesh, crunching – the thought terrified him and he closed his eyes. He had known these fears before, the harsh phantoms of withdrawal, shadows latent with menace and malevolent possibility, details ominous with malice; he began talking loudly to himself, telling himself that he had known these fears before, that they were all in his mind, that his flurrying panic was unfounded, that he should calm down, calm down, it was just the drink and they would soon be home. He tried to think of other things and his mind seethed with images, each one triggering off another in fearful succession – the doomed Bella, Langholm left to die on the road, the Crosbies quarrelling viciously in their house, the kids crying, maybe Crosby and Joanny had started fighting after they had left, maybe he had killed her, stranged her on the stairs or battered her to death as she tried to escape. They were all dying, everyone, all of them; he sensed this suddenly with a profound sense of his own frail brevity. One day they would all be dead, none of them would be left and this briefly complete life was nothing better than a glimpse into the dangerous dark, it was nothing, it was everything, it was running away, the roundabout out of control, the jig-saw falling to pieces. He stared out of the sidecar and saw the road and the trees hurtling by in a roar and his fear burst up again in a blaze; a feeling of suffocation seized him, a claustrophobic panic, the choked words of it climbing out of his throat, 'Langholm slow down, slow down you bastard slow down!' But Langholm could hear nothing, the flaps of his crash helmet, the roar of the engine and the wind and the perspex canopy were all barriers between them which McPhail's words could never cross. Completely unaware of McPhail's fears and dumb mouthings he kept the machine hurtling onwards into the night. McPhail scraped at the filthy perspex, and tried desperately to attract his attention but it was useless; Langholm like some huge indifferent power remained unmoved by all his fears and pleas; his goggled eyes were fixed ahead, unflinching, and his body and arms were rigid and unchanged. This remoteness inflated McPhail's dread and a feeling of sickness sprang from his fear – Langholm seemed suddenly to be hugely sinister, the embodiment of some evil, unstoppable, uncaring, never given to understand. He stared out into the oncoming road and saw there, rushing toward them along the light beam, a sparkling glitter like a spray of jewels, fragments flashing on the road and with a piercing shiver of fear he realised what it was – the half bottle of Langholm's which he had stolen from him and broken earlier on, its shattered glass now leaping towards them, the jagged edges flashing towards the wheels, the razor sharp pieces ready to slice and slash through the thin, bald rubber on the tyres. He wrenched frantically at the catches of the canopy, freed them and flung it open, the wind beating upon him, juddering the canopy, snatching at his hair and clothes.

'Hughie – the glass – the glass!' he screamed.

'What the hell are you doing Billy,' shouted Langholm. 'Get back in the seat – for fuck's sake get back in the seat or you'll cope the bike – you'll have us over!' Then abruptly they hit the glass and the machine leapt banging and skidding across the road, metal and stone screaming and scraping as they bounced and crashed amongst boulders and banks and trees and turf until finally, with a muffled, smothered boom, it burst into a whoosh of soaring yellow flames.

McPhail's eyes were open, and he was conscious of the flaring glow but he neither knew nor cared to know of its source; his consciousness was flooded overwhelmingly with suffering and he saw nothing and he heard nothing and neither did he remember the crash nor the houses nor the long roads of the night. Langholm limped painfully amongst the boulders and the now falling rain, calling out to him and asking could he hear, but he could make no answer and Langholm could not find him with the darkness and the glare of the fire in his eyes. It was only after a car had stopped and the people inside had come out to help that they found him; a dead fugitive in his last hiding place, his open eyes looking blindly back at them from his crushed skull and bright tears of rain tracing coldly down his cheeks.

VII
FIRES OF AFRICA

Naiwu Osahon

Photograph of Naiwu Osahon

The Nigerian media describes Naiwu Osahon as Nigeria's 'enfant terrible', 'angry young man', 'champion of the poor and exploited'. Naiwu sees himself as a cultural activist, artist, poet, actor, playwright and designer. He comes from Benin the famous ancient African empire of plastic arts, spent ten years in England from 1960-69 where he attended Leeds College of Commerce and Liverpool and Salford Universities, receiving a Masters degree in marketing from the latter. He is well known in Nigeria not only for his uncompromising stand against oppressive régimes, official corruption and rampant exploitation, but for his versatility as a painter, writer, actor, teacher, and designer including his unique tye and dye creations. Naiwu Osahon is the prime mover behind CANE, the Committee Against Nigeria's Exploitation. His many books include *The Climate of Darkness, No Answer from the Oracle, Black Power, The African Predicament, Sex is a Nigger, A Nation in Custody,* and he is the editor/publisher of a journal of the arts and letters called *Third World First*. He is currently based in Lagos where he has a large studio/workshop, and has travelled extensively in Europe and America.

FIRES OF AFRICA

Independence

Wait
>Listen
>>I can hear people screaming ...
>>screams of joy.
>The rains have stopped,
>>the war is over,
>>the blood suckers have laid down
>>>their guns.

But
wait, wait,
>don't turn your backs yet.
>>Devils are full of cunning ways.
>>Independence has ushered in
>>>neocolonialism

Who is going to teach my people
>the new tricks.
How long more before full independence
>comes.

Chaka is Back

There is smoke from chaka's palace to-night.
The air is rented by the witch-doctor's rituals.
I can see Balama doing the ogundigbo.
>it's the season of the yellow yams.

The dance of the seven deaths
The masks are every where
>our ancestors have honoured our call.
Salama is crying, the babies are crying –
>they can foresee but not foretell.

SILENCE

The chief's ward has arrived with a message.
        Ha! ha!
        White gods have arrived on our shores.
Kill them,
        the ancestors warn.

NO!
Welcome them,
        the chief directs.
                Let them have of our hospitality
                        and warmth.
                Give them the best we've got.

The visitors soon settled down to
                grab, grab and grab,
                giving in compensation
                the hoes and the bible.

The elders realised too late.
    ... if only we had listened
        to our ancestors that night.
    ... if only we had used our
        poisoned arrows in the first place.

Rapists

For centuries
        we laughed,
        sang,
        danced,
while lynchers stole our land.

We watched from our pens
        helpless,
        lifeless,
        drainted of emotions
while they raped our mothers
                        sisters
                            and
                        wives.

We even helped them mine
        our gold, oil and minds
        to enrich their cities and their lives

Fools that we were
    we let them rob us of life and dignity
    so to pass on to our children
    a history of fear docility and
        abject subjugation.

We've not been men enough
    but we owe our children their lives.

So let's rise now:
    an army of blackmen
    to win back
    life and dignity
        for the poor innocent black kids
        still being produced.

My country

I've a country,
    a very rich country,
                and
    I toil very hard for her,
    to keep her wealth in foreigners' hands.

I sweat all day long.
    to produce gold for European bosses
    who dominate our economy.

I work till I ache from exhaustion
    to make fortunes for Lebanese Gambists;
        and
I use my hard earned kobo
    to keep Syrian retailers smiling;
                and
                yet
                I
                can
                do
                nothing
    about the Indians in the forces.

But I ask:
    will my country ever reward me
    for all the effort I put into her
    if not as a black man, at least,
    as a son of the soil.

Bloody mother fuckers

My brother scrubbed
    white men's floor in Apapa
    to earn a cup of gari in cholera water,
    and engage a slow painful death
    till the ripe old age of seventeen.

I never met papa
    whom I was told had red fat eyes
    from crying 35 years till his
    heart packed up one early morning
    at breakfast.

Mama died on the job
    without giving me a chance
    to be a man.

Determined to have my own back –
    I busted school at 15
    took to the road,
    convinced of a living
    and a certain fame.
    Never having to scrub floors,
        shine shoes
           or
        carry the dogs food
        and
I soon was a man
a man at last,
        with
    the mother fuckers paying with every
    ounce of their blood to keep me alive.

Colonial bandits

You say
I had
    no culture
    no past
       You callous
          and
       misleading bandits.

If
all
I had were
    ancient
        Egypt,
        Songhai,
        Ghana,
        Bini,
        Mali ...
which of yours was a match.

Without a past
    how come I was so attractive
        to be colonized.
    How come you had so much of mine
        to loot and plunder.
    How come Picasso made a name and a fortune
        out of my abundance.

The C.I.A.

The
strategy
now
is
to flood American diplomatic missions
in Africa
with
trusted
black

C.I.A.
agents.

The natives are so stupid
they will
trust
any black face.

If America
were that honest
why
haven't they sent
Eldridge Cleaver
Bobby Seale
Huey. P. Newton
Angela Davies
here
yet.

Our oil

American
oil
will
last
her
several decades more.

Yet
she
sinks fortunes
        to dry out our wells.

Now that we still
        lack the technology
        and
        the knowledge of oil accounts.

All in a grand design
to keep us ever poor
and dependent on them.

Trusting in whites

Thousands
like me
inhabit
this
devil land.

    A city
    within a city.

    A mirror of our dejection
and
    before God,
our fate in the hands
of our fellow men.

Cartoonists

Their
cartoonists
portray
me
as a naked cannibal
while
they are lazing
    unadorned
    in aboriginal settings
gorging me raw
with their pens.

Cathedrals

Their god is money
we provide the rituals.
These days only the poor
and oppressed build
cathedrals,

the rich has the
world
at his feet.

The white lecturer

Some
weeks later
at a lecture
        the white lecturer was going on
about
        'African primitive tribes.
        ... Africans are untutored warriors
        ... they live on trees or in caves ...
        the cannibals molest white
        visitors ...'
he was going on.

I wondered
        how many of his relations had been
        served at my family dinner.

He didn't look particularly beefy
        himself, but perhaps his
        relations had been better bargains.

The chaos around me

What
is
there
to imitate
in
the
chaos around me.
The corruption,
infidelity and filth.
The world wars.

The hate I see
for me
on your faces
when
I shine
your shoes
        on
Sunday afternoons

Collusion

I see
the world
on a collusion course
mountains scald,
animals cremate,
vegetables incinerate
and
great big rivers seethe
and
evaporate into the thin air.

The world
disappears
into
a hollow nothing
and
man
is
responsible.

Dangerous man
is
hastening us to a premature doom
and
all we do now
is
wait
for
BLOOD TO FLOW

The solution

They are all out there
        every where dead
        without a song in their mouths
                a smile on their faces
                a name to bequest.

Dead like their ancestors before them
        captured, vanquished, destroyed
        yet, still immortal.
This black immortal race
so strong, so resilient.

The family

Every night
the family used to pray together
before going to bed.

Dad and Mum
used to sob a lot at prayers
and it was easy for me to join in
with them,
thinking it was the only way
we could reach God.

Dad used to offer
our bodies to God in prayers
and begged forgiveness
for our oppressors.

Suffering, he believed,
was a kind of passport to heaven.

I know better now.

A nigger of my own

A
Nigger
I'm
        I've witnessed
        the fires of repression,
        the bitterness of segregation
        and
        the inhumanity of racial discrimination.

A
Nigger
I'm,
        and I'm tired sick
        being a nigger.
        Tired to my bones like a nigger slave
        of a blood sucking plantation master.

A
Nigger
I'm,
        and I no longer want the molten uniform.
        How I don't deserve the rape and
        the persecution.

A
Nigger
I'm,
        a little too much
        never again to be nobody's nigger
        but my own.

Colour prejudice

Every time
a
blackman
is
humiliated

the
whole
race
is
humiliated
along
with him.

Who says slavery has stopped

They stopped
slavery across the seas
not out of love for the blacks.
Death duties were eating deep
into the pockets of the slave masters,
when
they could
just as well be
making
huge profits
enslaving us
in Africa.

The declaration

What chance have I
of ever winning
the whiteman's peace prize
when I have never known peace.
Bloody peace prize
to gag.
The prize of
infinite oppression
not for me,
I want to be a man.

VIII
THE SECRET OF THE
MOUSE-GREY ROOM

Tibor Várady

Translated from the Hungarian – Alan Duff

Photograph of Tibor Várady

Tibor Várady was born on 25 May 1939 of a Hungarian father and a Croatian mother, and writes in Hungarian. His wife is Serbian. He went to school in Zrenjanin, studied law in Belgrade and Harvard Law School. Since 1963 he has lived in Novi Sad and was one of the founders of the Hungarian language avant-guarde literary magazine UJ Symposium, becoming editor-in-chief in 1971.

He has published literary essays in many languages and won the literary prize Strazilovo, in 1979. *The Secret of the Mouse-Grey Room* already has an important reputation in Eastern Europe as a satire that amusingly and accurately catches the tone of modern ideological semantics in East European bureaucracies. He has perfectly caught the patterns of thinking and rhetorical style that typifies communist regimes and which he believes tend to be universal.

THE SECRET OF
THE MOUSE-GREY
ROOM

Tibor Várady

Translated by Alan Duff

JOHN CALDER · LONDON
RIVERRUN PRESS · NEW YORK

First published as a single volume in Great Britain, 1981, by
John Calder (Publishers) Ltd.,
18 Brewer Street, London W1R 4AS
and
First published in the USA, 1981 by
Riverrun Press Inc.
175 Fifth Avenue, New York, N.Y.10010

British Library Cataloguing in Publication Data

ISBN 0 7145 3842 6 Casebound
ISBN 0 7145 3843 4 Paperbound

Photoset in 11/11pt Baskerville by Specialised Offset Services Ltd, Liverpool
Printed and bound in Great Britain by Redwood Burn Ltd.,
Trowbridge & Esher

CONTENTS

OVERTURE

The conference-hall shall be mouse-grey!

Not light grey, not dark grey, not oyster-grey, not ash-grey, not dove-grey. Mouse-grey!

The decision was made by Vargas himself. The Executive Board had no say in it, may even have known nothing about it. On Sunday the painters set to work, and Vargas bought green-tinted sunglasses for the porter. Seen through green-tinted sunglasses, mouse-grey looks oyster-grey.

As far as the porter knew, green sunglasses were fashionable. Only now, when he crossed the red brick courtyard on his way back, he found that he could no longer distinguish the thin metal door-handles by their colour, and had to look whether they were turned towards the gate or the panel-wall (Some, of course, could be recognised by their rounded ends).

From now on, the rats and mice had to go by the difference in size.

It was indeed somewhat odd to submit these uniform ranks of handles to such an inspection. What worried the porter was that there might be nobody in the rooms behind. Though he might have remembered his friend, a colour-blind driver, who could not bear arriving first at the traffic-lights.

This had slipped the porter's mind. He was not, however, unduly distressed, when, after trying all the doors by rattling the handles instead of knocking, he still found nobody inside. He continued to be perfectly satisfied with his sunglasses, and this feeling dulled and helped to distance the otherwise disagreeable realisation.

Those attending the meeting had not even noticed that the walls of the hall had been painted mouse-grey. Their attention was focused rather on the oval table with its green baize cloth on which stood nine bottles of mineral water and DURALEX glasses.

The usual strained jokes were being exchanged. Rogers, after setting his briefcase on the table, sat down between Kavanomoku and Tilden and remarked that this meeting was getting off to an early start, which was tough on those who couldn't do without their afternoon nap. Kavanomoku and Tilden laughed. The opening gambit had been made, and this served still further to endorse the exigence of the joke-cracking ritual.

Hartmann, on entering, pressed the second of the light switches; the neon began to flicker, and soon there was a sparkle on the chrome of the tap above the washbasin in the corner. 'Mehr Licht,' Hartmann observed, most appropriately, and this brought a laugh from the others.

'Wer Licht?' retorted Jovan K. Milosević, playfully twisting his words.

'Ich Licht!' said Rogers, quick on his cue.

'Don't you think – Fair Licht?' quipped Mavrikis, coming in late with his repartee to Milosević.

'Or how about ...' boomed Vargas, twisting his moustache for a moment and looking around with self-assurance before capping them all with: 'Sehr Licht!'

(Vargas' contribution did not in fact qualify as a late-comer in this contrapunctal exchange. Two late arrivals = one arrival on time. Minus x minus = plus.)

'Mehr Licht,' observed Stanislas the porter – who almost never took the floor but rarely let slip any other chance for participation – groping his way back towards certainty.

There were by now some twenty-five people in the hall, and this might be considered a regular attendance. 'And here comes the quorum,' several of them remarked, to greet the arrival of a man in his sixties wearing a beret and spectacles.

'Dr Béla Quorum!' chortled Tsu Tao.

'Here's the quorum,' several voices repeated.

'Here comes the quorum,' insisted Stanislas.

A few more arrived and took their places. At the centre of the oval table, roughly seven metres long and four metres wide, a space had been left where more chairs could be placed. Professor Tashkalidze and Vice-President Hjalmarsson penetrated to the inner sanctum by crawling under the table; Ms Margit arrived by the overland route, skilfully negotiating the DURALEX glasses. Once they were all settled, Scattone – who had arrived first and headed straight for one of the inner-ring seats – handed them a box of matches so that they could set fire to the table. They were, so to speak, trapped in an artificial clearing – and the best way of fighting a veld-fire is to uproot the grass from a small patch around you, then light a fire on all sides which will drive back the bigger fire and destroy them both. A hair of the dog! as Scattone remarked several times.

The matches flared, one after another, but the green baize would not catch fire, and the only mark left was that of the black sideburns singed into the inner side of the table.

At 17.00 sharp, the meeting began.

Vargas took the Chair, stealing occasional (but proud) glances at the mouse-grey walls.

Four speakers came forward. They spoke reflectively – all at the same time, of course – but without any of that impersonal, somewhat weary concordance you find, for instance, with the Kessler sisters. And none of that monolithic unison chat. They always, however, managed to finish their speech(es) at exactly the same moment. Lawrence, Strezovski, Durrell, and Kappengut (sometimes spelt Kappenguth) were the speakers – the "Alexandrians" as they are called.

Their intervention was succinct:

'In connection with the question of the renewal of

livestock, there are two prevalent misapprehensions. There are those who claim that the re-stocking of game can be realised only through powerful state intervention, and those who contest that the re-stocking of game should be left to nature – wild trees must yield wild fruit. (At this juncture, Durrell and Strezovski looked right round the assembly.) Both assertions are extreme and therefore groundless. The truth lies somewhere in between.

'Just as with the electricity supply,' interjected Horváth.

Kavanomoku and Hjalmarsson considered that those people who believed that all human problems would be solved with the abolition of rent were wrong, but so too were those who thought that the abolition of rent would be of no consequence whatsover.

The majority of those present agreed with the 'Alexandrians'.

ALAVALAGANDA

Tsu Tao liked 45 rpm records.

This attitude concealed both a resoluteness and a nostalgia, the nostalgia being perhaps the stronger.

Tsu Tao fondly recalled the days of the Supraphon gramophones. There had even been a model which did not take 33 rpm records. This was a bygone civilization, which Tsu Tao had enthusiastically helped to build.

It still remained in his memory as a noisy, bustling age, in contrast to the present era of gramophones and amplifiers of tremendous accoustical strength. The appearance of the amplifiers put an end to the racket, and silence succeeded. It was also during the time of the 45 rpm records that classes at school became more homogeneous. Pupils no longer clung to their little cliques of four or five, but joined up in solid groups of twenty or more. Tsu Tao felt the winds of change. He tried harder and harder to integrate himself with the group: round his neck he wore a plastic disc on which was a golden violin. Then a plump flaxen-haired girl suggested he should read Kafka: he found himself wondering why the incomprehensible always had to be disagreeable as well. He pondered at length over this and once – delicately, so as not to appear provoking – even raised the question in public. It turned out that, apart from himself and the girl with the flaxen hair, nobody had read Kafka.

In Tsu Tao's recollection this age and civilization was preceded only by that of the 78 rpm discs, of which he had none but the haziest notions. It may have been on account of this that he never spoke of it, and also, perhaps, because in this age he was just beginning to perceive a (possibly somewhat bizarre) concept of which only the sketchiest outlines were as yet discernible: The Age of the Rubber Ball! This, perhaps, was the neatest formulation.

The rubber ball had turned up quite unexpectedly in a parcel from Holland, tucked away under second-hand – but welcome at the time – trousers and pullovers, squashed up against a cocoa-tin (leaving a dent he never managed to straighten out). It was a red rubber ball the size of an orange, with white stripes running round it. Tsu Tao spent all afternoon and evening bouncing this ball around his room. He tried to work out how high it bounced off the floor and how far it went if he deflected it off the wall. By the morning, he had already achieved something of the dexterity of a basket-ball player.

He bounced it down the steps and out into the street, zig-zagging among the passers-by. Nobody appeared to be disturbed by this, some did not even look round, and no questions were asked. This neutral balance was not upset until a lieutenant, leading his company off the main road, ordered his soldiers to form up in double ranks on the pavement so that they could watch the ball-bouncing Tsu Tao. Soon the ranks were swelled with passers-by.

Tsuo Tao deftly guided the ball among them, even managing to touch the white stripe each time.

A congregation coming out of a pagoda and a body of representatives from the local Assembly, together with clerks and petitioners, joined the ranks of the onlookers. The direction of his route was now channeled towards the Youth Hall of Culture with a prolongation down several rough-cobbled streets (in which Tsu Tao needed all his skill and ability to concentrate) and on towards the slaughter-house.

It was here that the first atrocities occurred. The slaughterers hauled their sacrifices out into the ranks of spectators; then, in order to have a pretext not to leave the spectacle, they began to slaughter them, slowly, so that they would not need to go back for new victims. It must, however, be pointed out – and this undoubtedly vindicates the slaughterers and other spectators – that the whole spectacle was more a cause of disturbance than of enjoyment, particularly since the bellowing of the animals in their death-throes rarely synchronised with the bouncing of the ball.

Past the slaughterhouse and over the yellow river was a grassy common, but here there was nobody standing around.

Tsu Tao was never again seen in the town. He recalls, however, that after this he did not see his rubber ball again.

This heroic age, now totally vanished, had nothing in common – as Tsu Tao knew full well – with the age of 45 rpm records, of whose atmosphere he had tried to recapture something for present times. Tsu Tao had two records, both 45 rpm's. On the one, Milan Vasilitch-(Nobby) sang a song called JULIANA; on the other, a West German record, the best number was one which ended with the chorus burbling ALAVALAGANDA, ALAVALA-GANDA, ALAVALAGANDA.

This afternoon he had again put on the Vasilitch record first. First he wiped it with a velvet brush, which his wife had made for him, then he plugged in the amplifier, checked the stereo speakers in each corner, released the arm of the record-player and let the needle gently down onto the record.

Tsu Tao returned to his armchair and sank back in it. With a barely visible movement of the head he followed the swaying of the paper dragons and Chinese lanterns hanging from the ceiling. As the first number was nearing its end and JULIANA was about to follow, Tsu Tao stood up, went over to the nearest plastic lantern (five or six of the lanterns were made of plastic, the rest of paper), took it down from the wicker-covered hook, and holding it in both hands went back to his armchair. Using his toes, he drew towards him the slippers he had left behind, snuggled into them, then raised the lantern with ceremonial deliberation to his lips.

He took his first sip of coffee at the very moment when the needle was turning in the blank space between the two songs.

Tsu Tao liked to drink his coffee from Chinese lanterns. (Every afternoon his wife filled the plastic lanterns so that they should be ready for him). Drinking coffee from the lanterns was more than just a mere eccentricity. There was in this act an impertinence, a defiance, which was enhanced by the fact that he did not turn it into a public gesture of exhibitionism but rather a private practice, a need, stemming from within and yielding inner satisfaction, enjoyed within the privacy of his own apartment. (The fact that he did also drink his coffee in front of guests in no way detracts from this. Tsu Tao frequently submitted his conscience to examination over this question, and each time reached the same consoling conclusion: that his sense of pleasure and defiance was not augmented by the presence of guests.)

In this gesture there was also a certain arrogant but wilful manliness, and a dazzling irrationality. If one was to try to find a comparable model of behaviour, undoubtedly the closest in spirit would be that of drinking-champagne-from-an-actress's-slipper.

This defiant manly spirit was augmented by the music. The song flooded out at full strength from the hi-fi set: JULI-JULI-AAAA-NA, JULI-JULI-AAAA-NA. Primitive men, swinging their stone axes as they circle round in the dance, the earth resounding to the heavy stomp of their feet.

JULI-JULI-AAAA-NA
JULI-JULI-AAAA-NA

This same fierce beauty was reflected in the Alavalaganda as well:

ALA-VALA-GANNN-DDAA
ALA-VALA-GANNN-DDAA

Tsuo Tao drank his coffees, one after the other.

And to himself he said, Alavalaganda, many times, one after the other.

Alavalaganda.

FIRST INTERMEZZO

(The integration of theory and practice)

Although this was only an informal get-together, some truly trenchant interventions were heard. The open discussion was held in Kavanomoku's office over coffee, mineral water, and even cognac. As is customary at such meetings, there was a consensus of opinion on all issues. The matter in hand was – as Kavanomoku personally stressed – 'whether today the classic distinction between theory and practice is no longer tenable.'

The contribution of Jovan K. Milošević was followed with particularly close attention.

Milošević had arrived somewhat late and, being unable to get one of the leather arm-chairs, was obliged to bring a seat for himself from the secretary's office next door. Leaning forward, he began:

'I should like to recount a small incident. It is of no exceptional interest – indeed, on its own, it might even be considered inappropriate here – but it does, I feel, nicely illustrate how widely informed people are of the integration between theory and practice. Last week I was down in Split. In the evening I had a train to catch and was hanging around in front of the station. As I tired of reading the papers, I started browsing through the time-table. There wasn't a soul in the street, apart from two women offering rooms for the night. They approached me several times because they saw me waiting around with a suitcase in my hand. I explained to them that I was travelling on, but they persisted in telling me how cheap their rooms were. There seemed to be no point in answering them, so I carried on looking at the time-table for steamers bound for the south and the islands.

Then a drunk latched on to me whom I'd like to tell you about. He was still a good way off when I first heard him shouting:

HAJDUK'S THE GREATEST TEAM IN THE WORLD
HAJDUK'S THE GREATEST TEAM IN THE WORLD

Local patriotism, of course.

When he came closer, I saw he was smartly turned out, in a checked suit with a neatly knotted tie that didn't slip down.

'I've got nothing against *Zvezda*,' he said, thinking perhaps that I supported a rival team, 'but Hajduk's the greatest in the world. The greatest team in the world! And Ivitch – he's a genius. The greatest trainer in the world! I know him personally. He's a great mate of mine. The smartest man in the world, Ivitch. Know him personally ... And d'you know why I think so much of Ivitch? D'you know why? *Because he's like Lenin.* That's right, Lenin. Vladimir Ilitch! No need to look so surprised – you heard me right. O.K., O.K., so I'm drunk, but I know what I know. And what I say – that's the truth. Ivitch is our Lenin. *He has integrated theory and practice.* Lately I've been reading the papers, and they all make headlines of it: theory and practice must be integrated ... Well, that's just what Ivitch has done! ... Following the path traced by Lenin.'

'I ought to add,' Jovan K. Milosević went on, 'that although the Hajduk fan was under the influence of alcohol, and his analogy was not only shocking but also in rather poor taste – I mean, comparing Lenin to a football coach, that's really going a bit far, isn't it? even if it *is* your favourite team – but I was interested all the same to hear that the Hajduk fan reckoned our newspapers were always making headlines of the need to integrate theory and practice. In the long run, though, they're right – these journalists and the Split fan – in spite of all their mistakes.

They've got an intuition, a sort of second sense, which tells them that certain truths (the eternal ones, in fact) which manage to break through with elemental force into public opinion, are actually characteristic of the life-pattern of the great men in history. Lenin, Danton, Beethoven, Tesla, Napoleon, Gandhi, and Nurmi have all forged the link between theory and practice. They did exactly what we too should be doing. At all events, I agree that it is in one's immediate environment that one should search for the appropriate model, for the concepts that transmit the thesis, and those that substantiate it.

'Apart from this,' Milošević continued, 'I gained nothing new from this conversation, although the Hajduk fan went on haranguing me for a good half hour. No doubt he had pestered several people before me who had told him to get lost, or had just walked off without bothering to hear him through – and I should probably have done the same if I'd had anything better to do. All the same, he was very friendly towards me. He could tell by my accent that I did not come from Split, which is probably why he kept assuring me that he had nothing at all against the Zvezda team. Each time, however, he would add that Hajduk was the best team. He also told me that, unlike Ivitch – whom he kept calling his friend – he himself was rather a man of theory. There was a time when he too could have played for the Hajduk first team, and even now he could have been in a better position, one such as I could not even imagine. But then, he was not a man of practice.

'On parting, he kept telling me he was going to give me a left-handed handshake, and he held out only his left hand. With drunks, you never quite know where you stand, though I think this may have been intended as a mark of exceptional distinction for me.'

After Milošević's speech, the assembled company drank another cognac all round. Then Kavanomoku announced that it would be a good thing to hold an open debate devoted to the topic of the integration of theory and practice.

THE GREEN NUTCRACKER

The green nutcracker belonged to the chiefs, which means that chiefs are all nutcrackers. This nutcracker was a green strip linking the chiefs with the outer world, but representing at the same time a dividing-line.

This green strip on the wall was also a mark of the divisions of time, termination and progression – continuity – not just the static mosaic of the unit of time, as was the horoscope beside it, on which the months did not mark their own sequence but were merely complementary (or independent) patches of colour. Running towards the green nutcracker, in the direction of the chiefs, the chiselled lines of the wall-panels led off into step-like blocks. Like the view from Rogers's old room facing the outer wall, on which the peeling plaster had left brick-red patches, marking the passage of the years as it flaked away.

The chiefs – some aggressively, others resignedly – were trying to demonstrate to the airport workers the possibility of a more complex juncture of time, despite the fact that their mandates were not concurrent.

While making love, Tilden's eyes had roved several times over the white plastic panelling of the wall – while Hilda was looking in the opposite direction, her eyes fixed on the alarm-clock – and he had several times come to the conclusion that the green nutcracker was of crucial significance. He found it easier to measure his fate by the nutcracker than, for instance, by the horoscope beside it. Tilden also attempted several times to let himself be swept up by a wave of lust and carried along on its crest, but not once did he succeed: the mercury column on the wall always rose to within a few centimetres of the green nutcracker-strip, where it came to rest and then slipped back.

Tilden had in fact met Hilda that evening at a dance in the students' restaurant. The tables had been pushed up against the wall, covered with coats and a clutch of girls who felt safer up there than down in the jam at the centre of the room. Most of the tables fell outside the range of the flashing strobe-lights. In these surroundings, Tilden was far from sure whether he would still find Hilda so attractive if they were to move to some more brightly-lit place.

It was Hilda who broke the ice:

'She can't be more than fifteen, if that,' she said, pointing to a scrawny singer with a frizzy Afro hair-do, who marked the beginning of each bar by leaping with a thump off the 20cm platform, then hopping back up again.

Tilden could not hear.

'Uh-huh,' he said. For a while he tried to work out what the woman might have said, then, feeling it was now up to him to take the initiative, he bawled out his suggestion that they go off some place where they could hear each other.

They drank a half-litre of red wine in a nearby café where the chairs had exactly the same green plastic covers and metal frames as those in the local trains. Between them was a narrow table, with a cone-shaped metal support in the middle. They sat facing each other. Hilda was blonde, with pouting lips. She was wearing a rather loose-fitting long yellow dress which gave her a plumpish look. For a while they chatted about the music; both agreed it was too loud. Tilden did not fail to use this opportunity of trotting out a not infrequently repeated fragment of his military past. There wasn't much you could tell him about noise, he said: after serving in the artillery he knew every conceivable dodge for protecting your ear-drums (it was a good idea, for instance, to keep your mouth open). But with music like this, even he was stymied.

'Tell me more,' begged Hilda, clearly struck by this revelation.

Tilden recounted a few more incidents from his soldiering days, including the one about the time when Mezernics one evening had set out his uniform in perfect order for inspection – his shirt neatly folded to precisely the same width as his trousers, everything spick and span. Only, the peak of his cap was facing towards the wall instead of the door.

'Whose uniform's this!' yelled the duty-officer.

'Mine!' said Mezernics proudly.

'I'll stuff your uniform for you!' roared the officer.

'Yes, Sir!' Mezernics replied, and in his confusion he saluted. Now it was the officer's turn to become confused, for this 'Yes, Sir!' had suddenly turned his threat somehow into a reality, as though he actually did mean to ...

Hilda was having a great time, and it was she who suggested they go back to her place for coffee as she lived quite close. On the way, Tilden gallantly swiped some flower-pots for her from the top of a stone wall.

The love-making part came up when, shortly after they had finished their coffee, Hilda produced an alarm-clock from her handbag and set it to ring 40 minutes later. She explained to Tilden that she reached orgasm after exactly 35 minutes, i.e. when the clock went off (allowing 5 minutes for undressing and warming-up).

Tilden continued trying to work out a regular time-rhythm on the wall, but this proved to be unfeasible because of the multiplicity of elements and possible combinations. The alarm-clock, however, like the neat parting down the middle of his hair-oiled scalp, split time in two directions. All that existed was either TOO FAR or TOO NEAR, and the two were separated by a hair-thin or, rather, dimensionless line.

The green nut-cracker still remained inaccessible: the doorless green wall of Paradise Lost.

This was perhaps the first time that Tilden had experienced no pleasure while making love. Although it did not put him into a particularly bad mood, but merely threw the bizarreness of the whole affair into stronger relief.

Dawn was breaking. They were hosing down the streets and mud was spattering onto the basement windows. Tilden stepped over the black hosepipe, overtook the water-cart, and turned left at the corner. As he was alone in the street, he took advantage of the opportunity to peep in through the windows. Inside one of the buildings, in a largish room, a chemistry lesson was under way: the sixth-formers, or perhaps they were university students, paid no attention to the gipsy girls going round from bench to bench offering carnations. After the lecture-room came several curtained windows, then a department store and finally the boulevard. Here a girl – quite shapely – crossed his path. Tilden recognised her from old times. Now it really was up to him, he felt, to make the first move. After all, they were alone in the street walking towards each other, and the girl was pretty enough to deserve the opportunity at least of giving him the cold shoulder.

'Want to go to bed with me?' asked Tilden wearily.

'Such an association presupposes love.'

'Love, to be sure.' Tilden was prepared to accept her attitude in principle. 'But love of what kind? Feelings are needed, but what kind of feelings? Criticism is needed but – I put it to you – what kind of criticism? And what, anyway, is criticism? Can it exist without self-criticism? Dare we venture so far as to believe that the humanity and the failings of others can be measured by the yardstick of our own positive egos, our high-aspiring probity, as flood water is measured by a water-gauge? And what do we do if the water overreaches the mark? Do we lengthen the gauge? Is it not a precondition of every criticism that we should first take the measure of our own frailty. Or that, in principle at least, we should own up to our own frailty? For, otherwise, how could we ever perceive the shortcomings of others. Like this, we can see them and even point them out. The self-criticism to which I alluded in my opening words is, hence, the basic requirement, the entry-fee one might say, which, viewed from a different standpoint, by revealing our faults renders us more appreciative of our virtues. One needs the mind of a Socrates to confess one's own ignorance. This we all know. And we also know that one must be of unshakeable virtue to own up to and lay bare one's own moral imperfections. What kind of criticism, then, is needed? And what kind of love? Is abstract love possible? Can true love exist without falsehood? And how are we to determine what real love is? By intuition?

'Confession?'

'Evidence?'

'Unanimous declarations?'

'Voting?'

'Democratic resolutions?'

'Unanimous democratic resolutions?'

'And while we're on to democracy, I support the idea that qualitative distinctions should be made within democracy. But what kind of democracy?'

Tilden was still firing questions when they reached the circular junction: the streetsweepers were laying the dust, and the first sharp rays of the sun were touching the outer grooves of this great disc.

The extirpation of responsibility and careerism: but what responsibility and what careerism do we have in mind here? Humanism – fine, but what kind of humanism? Freedom, but what freedom? And for whom? The freedom of the primaeval forest?!

His arguments proved to be convincing.

On that day, Tilden had two more sexual adventures. (It was he himself who described these escapades as 'adventures'. This word, he felt made the whole matter more acceptable and helped to detach it from the *perpetual flux*). Meanwhile he was reflecting on the utter senselessness of the Freudian concept that man's suppressed sexuality is constantly maintained in a state of sublimation, and that this is why men turn into scholars, or tyrants, or pianists, or financial geniuses. To Tilden's way of thinking, the whole idea would be just as logical the other way round. There are men who suppress in themselves the would-be pianist, banker or tyrant and seek fulfilment instead in a hyperactive sexuality. He for example had always wanted to be a singer, but had suppressed the burgeoning notes in him, and thrown himself instead into love-making. (Often as a result of his sublimating mechanism, but just as often out of a sense of propriety, for he felt that if he were to make no advances it might be taken as an affront, or at least an insult.)

Once, as he was methodically deflowering a 40-year-old virgin, Tilden was assailed by a ghastly thought:

'What am I? The Salvation Army?'

Unfortunately, however, he was unable to break with his established way of life.

TOTALITY

For several weeks, László Balogi had been ruminating over the problem of totality and the range of its possibilities. Sometimes he simply switched on the TV, the radio or transistor, and watched Belgrade, listened to Novi Sad, Budapest, the BBC, Sarajevo, Free Europe, Moscow, the Voice of America, and the feeling grew in him that the newcasts were becoming a tangible totality. He had experienced a similar feeling when the baritone sax had first been introduced in small jazz combos. At the time when most of the solos were taken by the trumpet, Balogi had felt a metallic manliness in everything, accompanied by a sense of discomfort – they always ended in sharp angles.

Basically, he still admired the trumpet-players (in spite of the fact that most of them had started out learning the violin, which perhaps could be blamed not only for their behaviour but also for their abrupt changes of personality). He admired them, and envied them as well – for their angularity. He long remembered the warm playful reproach Aranka had made to a trumpet-player as she snuggled up close to him during a break between numbers: 'Oooh, but your mouthpiece hurts! ...'

The saxophone solo was quite different. The tenor sax (and on the whole the alto sax as well) had more spleen – the melancholy of the wee small hours and the magic ability to adapt to the shape and internal disposition of the bar or night-spot. But what he missed was the trumpet's – sometimes rather jagged – outright manliness.

It was in the baritone-sax that Balogi saw the solution – a

total rounding-off, a combination of the laxness and malleability of the saxophone, and – though not quite in the same way as with the trumpet – something of that harsher manliness as well. A totality.

He now kept a constant record of such examples of totality, and gradually, like the pulsing flash of a glow-worm, the possibility occurred to him that he did not always need to choose between alternatives, and that dilemmas, contradictory values, social roles and relationships at work represented only one organic state of reality, which was susceptible to transformation and might at that very moment be undergoing change. It is one's outlook that must be altered – Balogi felt at times – or perhaps the outlook should be done away with altogether so that things might be experienced in their totality. Specialization has perhaps passed its zenith, and in the near future trained experts will be needed who are capable of viewing the flux in its totality. Perhaps not even experts. New trends, perhaps, will draw people closer together and break down the division between expert and layman. Our environment is ceasing to be a mosaic of narrow personal ruts and vast unknown territories, and everywhere becoming uniform and tangible.

These thoughts began to recur with greater and greater frequency, and so, when he was woken at four o'clock one morning by the telephone but got no response from the other end when he lifted the receiver, Balogi did not consider this non-response from the telephone as a hoax or a tasteless joke, but as a blow for anti-communication – the complement of communication.

Balogi felt that to reach totality he did not need to cover vast territories, that the distances could be demystified.

Many things, without any true reason – natural or social – but simply of their own accord, grow big and unfamiliar. It is the lawyers themselves who give inflated importance to law, philosophers to philosophy, diplomats to diplomacy. For instance, it was not on account of some remote primeval need for happiness or because of some recent inhuman tyranny that Stalin's police resorted to their great purges, incarcerations, and their attitude that 'behind every bush there lurks a spy'; it was chiefly for their own sake – to find a sensible and reasonable justification for the maintenance of their monumental apparatus.

One must, therefore, lay bare those dimensions which exist only for themselves, burst them like balloons, and immediately the world will become smaller, more comprehensible: men and their thoughts will enter into our range of contact and communication.

Balogi had genuine belief in the arts. He considered that Tolstoy was right in saying that Beethoven's Ninth Symphony did not unite men, apart from a select group which it set aside from the rest; but this obstacle, it seemed, could be overcome. He felt that some of the new theatre experiments, some poems, some happenings perhaps, or other forms of expression, possibly the classic chocolate-box pictures, or music, or even the Ninth Symphony itself (though for the time-being they may not have made this group substantially larger), did conceal other possibilities.

He often wondered whether artists were really capable of having a total relationship with the world, whether perhaps the jack-of-all-trades was capable, or nobody at all – because all activity was just specialisation, fragmentation. Sometimes, too, it struck him that perhaps through some (or all) of the professions or activities one could achieve completeness without having to hold all the reins at once.

This whole conglomeration of thoughts was still rather disturbing. Balogi repeatedly came to the conclusion that he was confounding different issues and that in his state of heightened interest he was prone to look upon everything that was of value to him or pleased him as a manifestation of totality.

He firmly believed, however, that he was basically feeling along the right lines and that sooner or later totality would emerge from behind the bounds of possibility.

On Sunday morning, as he set off on his usual stroll (this time he did not go without his beret and umbrella), he

found himself thinking that in fact totality and infinity
might well be akin. Like most of his classmates, he too had
been perplexed at the time (25-30 years ago) by the
question of whether there was an end to the universe, and, if
there was, what came after it. The conviction grew in him
that all forms of religion would be meaningful until
such a time as infinity and nothingness were rendered
sensible and tangible by science. Perhaps if he could break
through to thinking in total terms ... which for a few
moments he had once or twice succeeded in doing ... For –
as the newspapers say – Bobby Fisher is now a total chess-
player, and Ajax a total football team.

Balogi's route led him towards the tower and the
arcades. It was not raining hard, and his open umbrella
afforded him full protection; from under its cover he calmly
and methodically observed the people and the cars. He met
several young men, all of whom greeted him first. As he
passed what had once been the timber-yard he noticed that
there was still a vacant lot on the site of the adobe house
that had fascinated him as a schoolboy. Its walls used to
lean outwards, describing an angle of 75 or even 60 degrees
with the path. The windows had been boarded up.
Whenever he heard the saying, 'Never lean against a shaky
wall!' he had clearly imagined this house, which he had
always kept well clear of for that very reason.

He could not remember when it had been demolished.

When he reached the centre of town he walked past the
office in which he had first worked after matriculating and
where he had stayed on for three years. Only rarely did he
think back on those years. Strange to say, it was the
problem of meals that stuck most vividly in his mind. He
had never felt that the drawers of his desk belonged
sufficiently to him for him to be able to put his sandwiches
in them with an easy mind, still less did he dare leave them
on top of his desk. But inside his artificial leather bag they
absorbed an unpleasant smell. Worse still, they also turned
soggy. This, perhaps, is why Balogi cut out his snacks.

When he reached the arcades, he found many people he

knew gathered under them. Several of them used to hang about there regularly on Sundays; others came in to shelter from the rain. They were all armed with the Sunday papers.

For a good while they talked only about the rain, then Kappengut(h) moved on to sport.

'Tactically, our team's really well prepared – just they're chronically goal-shy,' he expounded.

'I always root for the better team,' said a red-haired young man with a neck-tie who had arrived by bicycle, holding the handle-bars with one hand and a darkish lilac umbrella with the other.

Durrell drew from under his arm a three-legged, leather-seated, folding hunting-stool, opened it out, sat down and gestured to the people round him:

'With regard to joint investment there are four distinctions to be made,' he explained, holding up his right index finger for a considerable time to emphasise the importance of the point. 'In the first instance, a capitalist country invests in a socialist country, but then a capitalist country can also invest in another capitalist country; in the third instance, a socialist country invests in a capitalist country, but then it can also invest in another socialist country.'

Durrell supported all this with concrete examples.

Balogi sensed that an interesting and meaty debate was in the making, so he suggested that they go and fetch chairs. Underneath the arcades there was a bank, and one of the group of Sunday-paper-readers – a man called Lodenheim, a maker of leather goods – happened to be on good terms with the porter. They brought out the yellow, angular chairs from the Board Room and placed them in a circle. There must have been about twenty-five people taking part, and they sat in two concentric circles. Only Durrell was slightly out of line, on his three-legged stool, which was lower than the other chairs.

The porter also joined them.

As soon as they had settled themselves, a woman rose to

speak. Balogi did not know her (nor, it seemed, did the others). She must have come without an umbrella, but probably not from far away, because she was not very wet. The jacket of her suit was not even soaked through, just dappled with glistening raindrops. With the nonchalant gesture of a female intellectual, she set her handbag down beside her.

'I've always said,' she began, loosening her head-scarf, patting her hair, then spreading the scarf over her lap, 'I've always said that it's better to tell people the truth to their faces than to try and smooth everything over.'

Balogi felt that the moment had now come for him to join in the discussion in order to render his attitude towards these questions more complex.

'I agree with all that has been heard so far,' he said, drawing his beret a little lower to protect him from the wind which was growing stronger and stronger, 'but I must point out that these are issues which cannot simply be settled overnight. Moreover, to be absolutely frank, I must stress that excessive procrastination could also be harmful.'

The majority agreed with Balogi.

The rain, meanwhile, was beginning to fall harder and harder, carried in under the arcades by the strengthening gusts of wind; the debaters tried to shield themselves from the squall by drawing the chairs closer together, but this was of no great help.

A young man in a green hat, called Ranivukovitvh, was the first to come up with a brainwave. He took out a roll of Sellotape and asked the people sitting in the two circles for their newspapers, and, by sticking the papers together in panels of four-page thickness, slowly erected a wall around the arcades. He was helped in this by the woman who had spoken first, by a pensioner who rarely had anything to say, by a young man in a yellow pullover with shoulder-length hair (nicknamed Netzer because of his huge feet), and by Durrell, who kindly left his stool. In constructing their wall they tended to keep the advertisements, TV programmes, and occasionally the stop press news facing inwards on the debaters, while the most important events in the political life at home and abroad faced outwards onto the street. This news-wall must have been a good two metres high. No space was left for doors, which meant that latecomers were unable to join them from the street. A great deal of sticky-tape was needed because otherwise the sodden patchwork of paper would have collapsed in a heap.

Kappengut(h) attended to the finishing touches. He took out of his pocket a KLICK-KLIPPER and ceremoniously removed the white aluminium cover so that the assembled company could gaze in wonder at the two parallel, beak-shaped steel cutters, with the needle-shaped incisor blade sticking out between them. Another gadget which Kappengut(h) always kept on him was the TELEREST, with which the KLICK-KLIPPER had more than a mere associative relation. Not only did these two devices more completely illustrate his outlook on life and his general comportment, from various angles, they also had an internal relation with each other, being physically complementary. Kappengut(h) always put the TELEREST first into his pocket, so that the KLICK-KLIPPER could fit neatly on top into the gentle curve of the semicircular rest. The two together formed an almost perfect square.

(Kappengut(h) had picked up the TELEREST in Canada during a trip he had made as member of a touring choir. If he did not want to hold the telephone receiver in his hand, or if his hand happened to be occupied – and to avoid having to strain his neck by trying to squeeze the receiver unnaturally between his head and shoulder – he simply fixed the gentle semicircular curve of the TELEREST to his shoulder so that, without any neck-cricking, so he could hold the receiver to his ear with only the slightest leftward inclination of his head).

Using the KLICK-KLIPPER he could snip out perfect square windows in the newspaper-wall with the greatest of ease. It should, however, be mentioned that the people inside were now able to see out only by looking over the paper wall because the window openings were blocked with the heads of curious by-passers. And, now that the rain had stopped, there were more and more spectators.

This exchange of ideas was followed by a shapely young girl with a rather large nose, wearing trousers and spectacles. Nadia.

'Nowadays there are more garage-mechanics than doctors. They worry more about the health of their cars than people.'

'Quite right!' said a silver-haired man wearing a silk scarf and a sailor's cap, known to all as the Captain. 'You've hit the nail on the head! And I should like to add to what you have said, because the situation is even worse than you describe, and we stubbornly refuse to recognise it. Industry today is run largely for its own interests. I repeat – for its own interests! It's becoming a myth, because it is invulnerable and serves only its own needs. We all know, don't we, my dear colleagues, what a thermos flask is. Not so very long ago it would have been impossible to imagine a journey without one. But was it really necessary? Not in the least. If it had been, we'd still be travelling with thermos-flasks today – but nobody does.

'If you will permit me, dear colleagues,' the Captain went on in his booming bass, standing up dramatically, 'I shall tell you a short tale. I beg the indulgence of those who may already have heard it. Well now, there was once a rich, gifted, and successful merchant who one day came across a fisherman dozing in the afternoon shade.

' "Why are you sleeping?" asked the merchant.

' "Why shouldn't I?" said the fisherman.

' "If you worked more, you'd live better."

' "How so?"

' "Well, to start with, you could buy yourself a fishing-boat. And if you worked even harder, you might even be able to afford a town-house, then you wouldn't have to live here in a hut by the sea, and if you ..."

' "Nothing but work all the time?" the fisherman interrupted.

'"Of course not. You could fix up a little place for yourself by the sea at weekends, and go there to rest."'

'"But why go to all that trouble when that's what I've got already?"'

The Captain brought his tale to an end with a great roar of laughter.

'Splendid story, isn't it, my friends? And instructive, too. All our lives we spend charging at windmills. Windmills! And meanwhile we run ourselves into the ground ...'

The majority of the audience marked their agreement with a dumb, melancholic shake of the head. A young man with striking blonde hair, visible moved, took out a 1/3 litre bottle of mineral water from the pocket of his windcheater, opened it, drank half, then took up the discussion.

'And how tiny man is in the cosmos ...' he said.

'Indeed,' replied the Captain, who was still keyed-up from his public appearance and had not yet returned to his role of passive listener although his speech was now finished.

Meanwhile, outside, on the other side of the newspaper barricade, more and more spectators began to gather, queing up in front of the windows. Those who were lucky enough to be right in front of a window were only willing to relinquish their positions for a bribe of several copies of the newspapers. This ruse enabled some of them to collect so many papers that if they had put them one on top of the other they could easily have taken up a comfortable kneeling position on them when their turn at the window came next. It now took longer and longer to get a turn at the windows, and the more impatient ones began to hack out their own windows – just large enough to poke their heads through. These new windows, though not as neat and practical as those which Kappengut(h) had cut out with his **KLICK-KLIPPER**, did nevertheless serve their purpose. (The amateur window-cutters simply used penknives or razor-blades, one even used a metal ruler.)

Thus about twenty of these one-man viewing-holes came into being, with the viewers' heads serving as illustrations to the newsprint.

Durrell took up the debate.

'I like simple people,' he said with conviction, 'because they're so honest.'

'Indeed,' said the first speaker, the woman who had taken off her scarf, returning now to the discussion. 'And I should like to add that it makes absolutely no difference to me whether someone is Serb, Hungarian, German, Romanian, English or Hottentot. What matters is that he should be a human being.'

Much nodding of heads: the Captain even applauded.

'What I'd like to say,' said Durrell, '– and this is perhaps a heretical thought, so let it go no further than our ears – but it is my personal and considered opinion that Thor Heyerdahl cannot be considered a scientist in the precise sense of the word.'

The replies were not slow in coming – and most were brief indeed. Only one person, a woman, spoke at length (about as long as the Captain had), with occasional interruptions to silence her little son. The gist of her speech was that she did not like people who spoke one way one day and another the next.

Balogi did not join in any more, but he followed everything with close attention and a pleasurable sense of excitement; and at the end of the meeting he helped to take the chairs back to the Board Room of the bank.

Then he set off slowly towards his office. He was still filled with the pulsating momentum of the recent events, and there was a purposeful spring in his step. Patches of lighter grey were beginning to appear in places where the tar had dried up, but the air was still quite fresh – a freshness sharpened by the PEPPERMINTS Balogi was sucking. He swung his umbrella with a lilt, breaking the rhythm now and then to describe a full circle in the air.

'My heart fills with the song
of tiny brushwood fires,'

Balogi hummed to himself the lines of the poet Ady, which he knew so well. He sensed that in this setting the words of the poem, with its autumnal tones, were slightly out of place, but it was not a chance association that had brought them to mind, for he did truly feel that tiny fires were flaring up all round him and he was caught by the powerful lyrical upsurge of the moment. In his mood, there was also a dumb nostalgia, invigorating rather than soothing, in the way a nostalgic song may be exciting to lovers. There was, too, in this mood (out of superstition perhaps) a suppressed delight and pride that things were at last under way, taking shape, moving finally towards completion. Unconsciously, Balogi intensified this impression by transposing the lines of the original from past to present. Out of context, the lines began more and more to take on the organic new meaning of their transferred setting.

'My heart fills with the song
of tiny brushwood fires,'

he sang again. Already they are burning within me.

Fires of all kinds smouldering softly away; energy waiting to be released – all that is needed is for the two poles to be brought together.

Now, perhaps, was the time to try to draw up his list. On this list all the alternatives, all the variants, would be strung together like beads on a necklace. Then, of its own accord, contact would be made and the circuit closed.

'My heart fills with the song
of tiny brushwood fires,'

Balogi repeated as he turned past the confectioner's shop into Constantinople street, where his company's offices were situated.

'Hi there! Woke you up, did I?' he called bluffly to the porter, though he was aware that this weak joke – no more than a drop in the ocean of weary wisecracks poured out daily at the main entrance and spreading out in a dreary shoreless sea – if viewed from another point of view might be considered complementary to the dried-up patches of pavement, the continuation of the movement his wife had made as she leaned over that morning to kiss him on his way out, or perhaps the outline of the idea sketched by the mineral-water drinker at the debate, the one who had alluded to man's insignificance in the universe.

Balogi climbed with youthful steps up to the second floor, walked in through the open office door, took a few reams of paper from the typist's desk (thin paper, because he did not feel like looking for paper of better quality) and without any head-scratching began to write out his *list*.

He felt that in the small straight marks he made there was a hidden curve and that if he were to join them together this inturning curve would gradually become evident; it only needed persistence for the point of contact to be reached and the circuit closed. Using an ordinary lead pencil, he wrote:

Suit, gents	1
clothes, working (gents)	5
tray, metal	3
case, attaché (leather)	1
towels	50
flag, national	1
flag, club	1
mineral-water bottles, lit.	23
tbl.cloth, embroidered	1
curtain, embroidered	1
container, metal	1
scuttles, coal	8
reports, bound	11
axe, large	2
cushion, feather	1
screwdrivers,	2
glasses (tumblers)	50
trays, plastic	3
fork, steel	2
coffee-cups, stndrd.	40
saw, hand-	1
lamp, oil	10
welding-torch, 350 W	1
jugs, water	4

glasses, sherry & liq.	10
trousers, unlined	1
stamp, rubber	2
stamp, circular	3
padlock	2
mouse-trap	1
carpet, strip-	46m.
shoes, ladies	11prs.
ashtray, ceramic	5
wall-plug (stndrd socket)	4

Space left for additions, then signed:

László Balogi – Laci*

*By his friends he was known simply as Laci

SECOND INTERMEZZO

(Let's speak openly)

After the meeting they again met in Kavanomoku's office for a small informal gathering. Kavanomoku ordered six coffees straight away (Durrell did not want any).

The discussion naturally revolved around all that had recently taken place, and Horváth did not fail to observe that Kismárton said only 'Ah-ha' and thrust forward his red nose when it was pointed out to him that the matter in hand was the grounds for defrayal.

'All he said was Ah-ha,' the others repeated discontentedly.

Theo Butor then pointed out to these others that what he personally had said was dum-dum like that; he did not consider himself competent to deal with this particular question, but even if he were, he very much doubted if he would be able to adopt the position which Tsu-Tao and Kismárton were defending. Dum-dum – no nonsense.

Kavanomoku went on to say that certain persons spoke for too long and without sufficient openness, and that certain ideas were beginning to circulate which, if they were to be credited, advocated a thorough spring cleaning in the office – and no doubt elsewhere as well – while in his opinion they ought to be sticking to the well beaten tracks of the revolution.

To the sounds of unanimous approval, coffee was served.

After a short break, Hartmann took the floor. First of all, he announced his support for the viewpoints already expressed, and stressed in particular the importance of openness in speech.

'Let us speak openly,' Hartmann continued. 'We ought somehow to set up the beginnings of a new structure – found a club, perhaps. It goes without saying that we could envisage only an institution into which the right of entry would be strictly reserved, as, for example, the Olympic Champions Club, or, I venture to suggest, an association of those who have never suffered from any consuming passion, or of those who for at least a year have not had a single day's absence from work. Please understand that I mention all this only by way of example. What really matters is that the conditions of entry should be strict, because without restrictions the self-esteem of the members is undermined and the quality of the membership suffers too. What is essential is that it should be difficult to keep up with us. First we must set about the construction, then attempt to catch up with ourselves. It's as with decorations, or the conferring of honorary degrees, or doctorates, or let's say membership of an Academy or of a Board of Directors. First we must set up the Board, then catch up with it. I hope I am making myself clear. First we must hold back a little, then, as it were, sprint forward until we are pressing on our own heels.

'There is no other choice open to us,' Hartmann continued, 'than to press on with the matter and keep striving forward. If you will excuse a somewhat banal illustration, animals – at least, dogs, have no need to go to these lengths: there's always somebody around to throw a stick or a rubber bone for them. Then all they have to do is chase after it. We, on the other hand – to return to our former proposition – have to throw the stick *and* chase it, we have to form our own club. To begin with, there should be only the club: it would be best if for at least one year we had no members at all. This, of course, would be assured by our exclusive conditions of entry. In time, somebody would succeed in meeting the requirements. This might be, for instance, Kavanomoku.'

'No matter who,' Kavanomoku interrupted.

'Certainly, that's not the most important, though I

venture to think that such a choice might still be best,' Hartmann added, and Kavanomoku did not make a second intervention. 'Later, we would gradually succeed in incorporating the others. Again, we would be pacing ourselves.'

Approval was not slow in coming, though expressed with somewhat more than the customary reserve. The reaction was more animated, however, when Durrell smilingly remarked that there was one quality in Hartmann he dearly liked – that he was always such a great guy.

Horváth once again brought the discussion back to the point by recalling that when Kismárton had been informed that the matter in hand was the grounds for defrayal he had merely thrust out his red nose and said Ah-ha.

THE SONGSMITH

Ms Margit several times told the story of how she had travelled with the nationally famous centre-half. She had sat beside him in the aeroplane on the three-seat side. The window seat was occupied by an elderly man with a white moustache, who did not remove his hat; in the centre seat was the football star, and on his left Margit.

'I didn't recognise him at first,' said Margit. 'He was wearing a dark suit, white shirt, black tie, and a mourning-band on his lapel. He fell asleep even before take-off, or at least tried to sleep. First he leaned forward, propping his head up with his arms on his knees, then he leaned back. He tried every position, including my shoulder – and didn't even apologise. As if he could do just as he liked! But I wasn't sure it was really him until we were getting off the plane and somebody called him by name. The nationally famous football-star smiled and waved back; it was only when the person in question broke through the crowd and came up to offer his condolences that he dropped the smile and grew serious. The football star, you see, had just returned from his mother's funeral.

At the airport bar the centre-half drank a cherry juice and two coffees. One more than Meursault, he thought to himself. (Over the last two years, the nationally famous football star had been suffering from constant injuries, and had put in a good deal of reading.)

But their situations were not quite the same, because Meursault had drunk one coffee at the death-bed and another after the funeral. Because he was dog-tired.

There was, after all, a difference. Camus had given a somewhat grotesque twist to everything. Perhaps in the fifties that was how it had to be done. So many things today were different. And even if I did drop off during the funeral dinner, it still doesn't mean I'm going to bump off an Arab. Then you've got Plarr as well, in *The Honorary Consul.* He didn't get worked up about his mother either. I never had any trouble with my mother. The only thing I couldn't take was when those imbeciles in the club started the big-grief act and all the phony distress symptoms that go with it. The coach even tried to make us believe it was a tragedy for the whole club if the team-captain's mother died. Why a tragedy? Because the captain would be out of action for a week? I couldn't have played anyway – because of my ankle. It may never even get better. Maybe my time's up. Got to make way for the young.

After all, Plarr managed to get along somehow with his mother – and to go on sleeping with his friend's wife without getting all tied up in knots about it. Not even when they kidnapped his mate by mistake and his life was in danger. Plarr even helped in a way with the kidnapping. But he was still a decent sort. And when he got tired of his friend's wife, he just gave her the push: no heartaches, no 'machismo', as Greene would say. No grand gestures and no canny 'take-offs' when he had to visit a sick-bed or his barber, no puffing out the chest (like a sprinter coming up to the finishing-tape) when he went to see the friend whose wife he had been laying. He just went his own sweet way, without wasting time on shamming grand farewells and photo-finish arrivals, and getting everything all mussed up. If Clara phoned and he didn't feel like going round, he didn't go. He didn't feel the need to be constantly proving himself, to be burning, yearning for what he's got anyway. Play up, play up and play the game! Not always groaning and grovelling on the ground, trying to whip up a bit of excitement, then hanging on with fresh ferocity until someone brings you a cropper again, or else dragging through with the game at the same half-hearted pace, keeping a stiff upper lip, your soreness ennobled by the tense restraint of your regard: You-tripped-me-up-but-see-if-I-care.

Plarr's was in fact the true, pure, modern love. Moving at its own pace, doing no more than necessary. Meursault was perhaps to some extent truly '*l'étranger*' – Plarr no longer, though he was something of a Camus figure. He had matured; he no longer kicked against every petty regulation. Or perhaps men as a whole had matured, with their petty regulations. Plarr was just a normal man – anyone who reads the book cannot help but feel this – in the same way as it is normal for me to take a nap or have a coffee. I've been travelling all night; couldn't get a plane on the way down. If I'd been able to get a plane, I wouldn't have dropped off during the speech. It's as simple as that. I never had any trouble with my mother. Meursault also behaved differently when it wasn't so sultry and after he'd had a good sleep. You can't spend your whole life standing to attention.

On arriving at the centre of town from the airport, the football star of nation-wide fame took a look at the posters. It was a warm May day, and some men were already in shirtsleeves; he, however, did not feel too uncomfortable in his dark suit. After a sleepless night he usually felt cold.

JEREMY DURST – one poster read. Durst, the SONGSMITH. Half past seven in the amphitheatre of the Mechanical Engineering Faculty. The whole pillar was covered in DURST posters. Some had been torn off.

'Who is this Durst?' the football star asked of Hjalmarsson, who was leaning against the pillar. He was wearing only sandles on his feet; the zip on his jeans had opened a few centimetres at the top. Hjalmarsson had been a classmate of the football-player. Now he was a sculptor. But nobody knew how he earned his living.

The centre-half recalled that Hjalmarsson had once told him that artists, too, can assume off-the-peg personalities, depending which bandwagon they decide to jump on. That's why the sculptors suddenly vanished into thin air:

nobody wanted to hear of sculpture as a profession. It degenerated into a side-kick of painters. He, Hjalmarsson, had sworn never to dabble in any other profession or art-form. The football star had fully approved at the time. On the whole, he felt that Hjalmarsson was always right; even when once, while they were still at school, Hjalmarsson had argued that 'if you like a woman and you don't ask her straight away to sleep with you, then you'll end up marrying her.' And later, the football-player had often repeated this thought as his own, without ever contesting the clear evidence to the contrary, i.e. that he had already encountered many women he liked, without immediately making this proposition to them, yet he had not married a single one of them. (Moreover, he *had* asked his wife the same question right away, and during the first days of their acquaintance could keep his eyes on nothing but her thighs and her backside underneath the body-hugging white woven dress.)

Another of Hjalmarsson's principles in which the football star believed without requiring proof was that: 'the only thing you need to know is that what is beautiful is true and what is true is beautiful. And that's enough.' Hjalmarsson was quoting Keats, of course, much as he always cited somebody – some French author – when dropping an axiom about women.

Often, too, he recalled the sculptor's jazz-period, and the conviction they had shared that jazz was the summit of music. They used to spend evenings at Hjalmarsson's listening on a bad radio-set to Wyliss Conover, their ears pressed against the wooden slats of the speaker. Most of the time, the radio spluttered and crackled, but sometimes for a few seconds the tone was as clear as if the jazz-group had been right there in the room. Then the station would be lost again and they would tap and rap desperately at all the old 'weak-spots' on the set in their attempt to get back the sound. It was also during the jazz-period that their parting occurred. The football-star had the feeling that Hjalmarsson's fingertips had not been yellowed by nicotine but by the wooden slats on the radio and that – as he argued to himself – he was turning into the same kind of man as a collector of insects or Dinky-toys. On the other hand, Hjalmarsson told him straight to his face that he, the football-player, was voluntarily hiding his head under a candle-snuffer and shouldn't be surprised if he found himself gasping for air. (The centre-half, oddly enough, believed in this observation as well, and soon began to see himself as destined to live a candle-snuffed life, although he did not yet feel himself panting for air.)

His favourite memory was, however, of their conversations by the sea-side, which must have taken place during a school outing. They had strolled among the pine-trees, with the sea only a few metres away. Chains of caterpillars were trying to cross the rough stony path before being crushed by passing feet. They guessed that the one in front was some kind of leader, and wondered what would happen if they were to crush only him. But for some reason they never got round to this experiment. Hjalmarsson had talked about the trees on their right which grew horizontally, straight out from the shore over the sea. According to him, the sea exerted an attraction on the trees, or the sea and the moon together somehow, so that they were drawn by the rhythm of the ebb and flow – down, back a little, then further down. Or perhaps the trees were simply dizzied into this horizontally from gazing and the moon and the stars in the water. Like somnambulists. Or like those who, with the waxing and waning of the moon, turn to killing, strangling, and other crimes of violence. It may be that murderers, gradually, over many years, advancing with a smooth throbbing rhythm, recoiling, then advancing again, are still restrained by many ties and bonds which are never severed, never broken, but grow instead more distended, tauter, thinner, finer, until the moment when they no longer restrain but rather accompany this forward impulse, becoming thin as air, the air which the killers breathe in at an ever-quickening pace. Then comes the instant when the forward swing comes to its limit, the end of the tether is reached, all movement ceases, and there they stand free and erect like an exclamation mark before the victim.

For a long time Hjalmarsson and the football-player had gazed at the almost completely bare trunks of the trees leaning out parallel to the surface of the water. Under what sign of the zodiac might this tree have been born? Hjalmarsson wondered.

'I don't really know who this Durst is,' Hjalmarsson, leaning against the advertising pillar, admitted to the centre-half. 'I don't really know, but he's sure to be one of that yeh-yeh lot; though his lyrics might be a bit better since he works on his own. These types all come along with their Bob Dylan tricks. They think they're the chroniclers of their time but they haven't got the patience to let things grow inside them until they've got a message worth delivering. Every little incident in their lives with the merest hint of drama is immediately whipped up, ripped out of the loose-leaf notebook of their experience and flung into the air in the hope that the wind will catch it. Their hair is long and they all wear semi-uniforms, like postmen.'

They decided in the end to go to the Songsmith's concert. The centre-half lived nearby, right in town, so they went off to get his car. 'The FIAT always needs warming up, even in summer,' said the football player by way of apology for the waiting. Then, with the horn blaring, he drove out through the covered gateway. On reaching the pavement, he slowed down, then roared off with a screech of tyres onto the main road. Suddenly, on the edge of the pavement, Ms Margit appeared from behind a kiosk. At the very last moment, the football star managed to slam on the brakes.

'Stupid woman,' he exclaimed, though not with any great conviction, more as a comment to Hjalmarsson. But Margit gave as good as she got. She, too, seemed to find the word 'stupid' most appropriate for her retort, though perhaps for other considerations than those which had moved the football star to speech. It was consciousness of guilt that had suppressed the former's inner-swelling polemical rage (the close shave had, after all, occurred on the pavement); Ms Margit, on the other hand, was intent on preserving her femininity, which was why she settled for this bland, practically meaningless word (reserving the meatier, harsher, more earthy expletives for her own internal satisfaction). In her subsequent words, however, Margit gave vent to this harshness and earthiness by asking the football player if he thought he could now do what the hell he liked, going around killing people and getting off scot-free. And did he think he was the most important person in the country? (She avoided saying the most important 'football-player' because she felt that this would be an admission of a somewhat humiliating one-sided acquaintance.) You seem to think, Margit went on, that just because you've got a dirty great car and you can step on the gas you automatically know how to drive. Knowing how to drive properly means even more to a man than his virility. But believe me men don't understand anything – this, that, or the other. They haven't a clue.

'Idiot,' the football-player muttered several times after he had finally succeeded in shaking off Margit. But when he turned into the Mechanical Engineering Department, he had to admit that fundamentally Margit was right in saying that although men set great store by their virility, it is even more important for them to be good drivers.

'Strike another match,' said the young man at the door when the centre-half asked him if they had to buy tickets. The football player stopped, puzzled, then followed Hjalmarsson who was striding confidently into the amphitheatre. The front two rows of seats were empty, but there must have been about seventy people altogether, scattered about the hall. Some were slouching cross-wise on the flip-back seats; one girl, in jeans and a blouse, was lying on the floor. Nearly all of them had their feet up on the seats in front of them; many were barefoot.

'In our days it wasn't the thing to go around barefoot: we had waxed floorboards – no parquet for us. You just try walking barefoot on waxed floorboards,' Hjalmarsson kept muttering, as they looked round for a place to sit. In one row a short-skirted blonde girl was sitting by herself. 'D'you mind?' the football-player pointed to the seat beside her.

'Strike another match,' said the girl, turning her head away. But then she looked back for a moment at the centre-half's dark suit, his white shirt with its washed-out design, and his mourning band.

On the stage, a couple of people were fussing around with the mikes. It must have been around eight o'clock by now. 'Won't keep you long – just a little patience till we get this bugger fixed,' said the one with the longest hair. He had a hawk's nose, and was wearing a high-collar Cossack-style shirt and green trousers: Durst, no doubt.

'Strike another match,' suggested some of the audience.

'What's all this match-striking about?' asked the football star, leaning over to Hjalmarsson.

'Some Bob Dylan gimmick. Strike another match! It's a kind of cool romanticism – low-key boasting. Don't get uptight about anything. If it doesn't work, strike another match – maybe it'll catch. If one job doesn't work, try another. It's not the job that matters. If one woman leaves you, another'll come. You don't like one town, go to another. Or another country. Another planet. If you don't like the boss shouting at you, just quit. Find another – till he starts yelling too. Or don't look for any boss – let them yell at their desks. If your writing doesn't work, try painting. Or playing ducks and drakes. Or not even that. Life won't make a fool out of you!'

Shrug your shoulders, cup your hands, and strike another match right along the side of the box.

... It used to be long blonde hair + candle-light; or a wide deserted street – you're wearing a dirty white windcheater, upturned collar, from behind dim lights a piercing

saxophone solo padded by a bass backing; or alcohol
(which this bunch consider passé) – hair tumbling over
your forehead, you look up but your eyes don't focus on
anything: clearly you've got some important forgetting to
do; or – shirtsleeves (hair on forehead again), stubble on
your chin, shirt unbuttoned at the neck, tie pulled down:
someone near you asks if you've really been up all night at
the typewriter, and you make no answer; or – you look
round coolly and take a slow easy breath, although you've
got only five minutes left till ...; or – you announce that
you've come to bury Caesar not to praise him, or that
personally you have no bones to pick with comrade
Ujfalusi ..., or that you are aware of your own
shortcomings; or, like Baudelaire, you say:

> Gentle reader, calm, bucolic,
> Solid, simple, honest man,
> Throw away this vicious volume
> Dissolute and melancholic.

Something like that, anyway. Strike another match.

The centre-half agreed.

Meanwhile, the amplifiers had somehow been set up.

'One, two, three; testing, testing, testing ...' said the
Songsmith, trying them out. 'Got these shits to work at
last ... (laughter). Dunno why you bothered to stick
around – I'd have buggered off ages ago ... (pockets of
laughter). Anyway, I'm not going to waste any more time –
let's cut the cackle ... Haven't even let the organisers
introduce me ... (the organisers smile). Guess it's best if I
just start, so – let's take it, man ... Just wanna let you know
I'll be offloading my own stuff on you ... (patches of
laughter) ... And I'm gonna begin with the one I wrote last
... so the last shall be first ...'

The Songsmith checked his tuning once again, strummed
a few trial chords, then started to sing:

> O LORD LET ME BE SIMPLE
> A PEBBLE AMONG PEBBLES
> O LORD LET ME BE SIMPLE
> A PEBBLE AMONG PEBBLES

O LORD LET US BE ALL ALIKE
SO YOU CAN LOVE US ALL ALIKE
O LORD LET US BE ALL ALIKE
SO YOU CAN LOVE US ALL ALIKE

O LORD PERFORM A MIRACLE
TO END ALL MIRACLES
LET US ALL LIE UPON THE ROAD
AND LEAVE THE WORLD BEHIND US

LET US ALL LIE UPON THE ROAD
AND LEAVE THE WORLD BEHIND US
AND REACH TOWARDS THE RUBY LIGHT
THE RUBY LIGHT OF PEACE

'Good stuff,' said a young man to his neighbour, who was lolling back with his feet hooked over the seat in front. (The only sensible posture to come out of the business culture, as Hjalmarsson later informed the faithful.)

'Good words,' came a woman's voice from further down.

'It's not a revolution he wants, just peace,' suggested the football-player.

'Not even peace, just that everyone should be left in peace. The two are not the same,' replied Hjalmarrsson.

The flaxen-haired girl beside them rose to speak:

'I LIKE THIS SORT OF THING. RUBY PEACE,
WHERE THE YELLOW SUBMARINE TAKES
YOU TO.
AND I LIKE PRÉVERT AS WELL. BOTH
BOOKS.
PAROLES AND HISTOIRES AND THE
OTHER ONE.
AND TOM JONES, BECAUSE
HE ISN'T LIKE THE REST.
AND TAGORE.
LONG WALKS BY MYSELF.
AND THE SUN, DAYS OF SUNSHINE.
NAIVE PAINTERS.
AND REAL HUMAN CONTACT.

'Yeah, yeah – all that,' a number of voices were heard: some had to show they shared her sentiments, others let it pass. Let everyone do his own bit. Tagore Tagore. Tom Jones Tom Jones. If you want to go barefoot – do. In mourning – in mourning. Strike another match ...

'AND I PROPOSE WE VOTE ON IT. EVERYONE THE WAY HE WANTS, THE WAY HE FEELS ...' the girl went on.

'LET'S VOTE!' came an excited shout from the back. It was Stanislas, the caretaker, who had been standing in the doorway and now came in to sit down in the front row.

'All right! Let's vote!' said the Songsmith, taking over again. 'All those in favour – reach for the sky!'

Most of them, with a nonchalant tilt of the head, raised their hands right up from the shoulder and voted. Durst counted 28 hands.

'Those against?' Nineteen.

There were twenty-two abstentions.

Durst and the organisers decided that the voting was not quite regular because the votes, if added together, came to slightly more than the number of people in the audience. (The reason was clear: Stanislas had been carried away and raised his hand in favour, against, and in abstention.) The Songsmith pointed out this irregularity, but hastily added: 'Who cares!' and, 'I mean, you're not going to get uptight about all this crap, surely!'

'Strike another match,' came the cry from all sides.

'We need urns. Proper voting is done with urns and little balls,' said a young man wearing a scarf.

'And guitar-strings stretched across the inside of the urn,' the Songsmith added, 'slanting downwards so that the balls bounce from one to another, like hopscotching on a staircase, picking out the three songs: IN FAVOUR, AGAINST, and ABSTAINING. Those three. The Lilliputians had only two, which is why they couldn't manage without Gulliver.'

'Hear, hear! Long live the vote!' came the shout.

'Then let's celebrate!' the Songsmith yelled into the

mike. 'All together now – singalong with me!'

The whole amphitheatre joined in the refrains, swaying to the beat (like negro Gospel-singers, as Hjalmarsson put it).

SOME ENCHANTED EVENING
YOU MAY SEE A ...

After this number the distribution of votes was much as it had been on the first occasion.

THIRD INTERMEZZO

(The Songsmith's Encore)

The petit bourgeois is made up
purely of 'on the one hand'
and 'on the other'. (*Marx*)

'I don't like it when Lawrence runs the meetings,' Arak
declared at one of their customary informal get-togethers. 'I
don't like it because he leaves no room for a good friendly
exchange of views – he's always trying to rush things
through with a majority vote. As soon as there's a difference
of opinion, he immediately calls for a vote. You have to be
constantly on the ball. You can't look away for a second
because as soon as your back's turned the heads go up and
when you look round again you've no idea whether they've
reached the in favour, the against, or the abstention. With
Lawrence you have to be on the ball the whole time.'

Kavanomoku pointed out that there were nevertheless
occasions when this way of voting performed a useful
function, particularly when a demonstration of unity was
required.

'Furthermore,' added Lyertovsky, 'voting has become
widely accepted by the people.' Then he continued as
follows: 'If you will permit me, I should like to relate to you
a most interesting incident concerning this matter. The
other day, we were walking back with Eftehari from the
General Weights and Measures Board, and, as the weather
was particularly pleasant, we made a slight detour towards
the university campus. Being a true nature-lover, I was
admiring the willow-trees, and it was only after Eftehari

had spoken that I became aware of the sound of some kind of music, or, as Eftehari wittily put it, 'hulabaloo'. The sound seemed to be emanating from the Department of Mechanical Engineering, so, as we had plenty of time in hand – the Board meeting having taken somewhat less time than expected – we decided to look in.

'Although we followed the sounds, we still did not manage to find our way quickly to the source of the 'hullabaloo' – to quote Eftehari – because Efethari had set off down a corridor in which all interleading doors were locked. Nor did we meet with anyone who might have put us back on the right tracks; still, we did manage to get there in fairly good time. The music was being made in one of the ampitheatres, and we were astonished to discover that all this sound was being produced by one man.

'I should also mention that all those in the audience, with the exception of a young man in a dark suit, were dressed in the most tasteless manner. They were, however, listening with rapt attention to the songs. Nor did they remain merely passive listeners: after each number many of them freely expressed their opinion, then voted.

'Voting was even brought into one of the songs, and after this I felt it was up to me to join in the debate. Eftehari agreed that this would be an excellent idea.

'I should not like to bore my listeners at this moment with an account of the full details of my speech. What I particularly stressed was that on the one hand there were those in whose opinion voting should be completely eradicated from social practice, and on the other hand those in whose opinion decisions should always be reached by voting – the voice of the majority. After clearly demonstrating that both points of view were equally untenable, I thought it fit to point out that there were also two approaches to the question of defrayal, on the one hand and on the other, neither of which led to a satisfactory conclusion.'

'I shed light on several more issues,' Lyertovsky continued, 'but as I have already mentioned, I should not

Tibor Várady

like to weary my listeners by recounting in detail what is already familiar. This I prefer to do on a more appropriate occasion, for in the present circumstances it would, I think, sound out of place. I should however like to stress – and here Eftehari agreed with me – that they engaged in the discussion most actively, and with utter spontaneity, which is also important. There were countless interjections of approval, and the audience demonstrated its appreciation in an unusual but truly natural way: the great majority of those present leaning forward then back with a gentle swaying rhythm, all together.'

'Forward-backwards,' Hartmann suggested as a more concise formulation.

'Yes, all swaying together,' Lyertovsky repeated, 'with a blissful smile on their faces. I remember one young man in lilac coloured jeans turning round to ask a flaxen-haired girl if she felt this wonderful, smooth see-sawing motion, *on the one hand* and *on the other*, this way that way, neither one way nor the other. As somebody else said, it was pure folklore – the genuine thing.'

'I found it particularly interesting that when I came to hear their opinions on the question of defrayal, the performer himself remarked that he was particularly taken with the word itself – *defrayal* – because it sounded like a smooth mossy stone.'

'Defrayal ...'

'Defrayal,' the others repeated.

'And to conclude,' said Lyertovsky, 'I should like to emphasise that when it came to voting, a convincing majority was in favour.'

THE HOLY OFFICE

Lawrence and Vargas made off in the direction of the river. It was getting on for four in the afternoon, but they knew full well that the Holy Office was still open at this time. They also knew perfectly well that others were setting out for the Holy Office from various parts of town. From time to time, Lawrence switched on his walkie-talkie to make contact with Horváth, Strezovski and a young woman whose name he did not know, but whose husband's Christian name was Helmuth.

When they reached the street after the grove, they were alone. There was not even a parked car in sight. Lawrence and Vargas were revelling in their newly-earned freedom. After crossing the dusty green strip of sparse grass separating the pavement from the road, they came out onto the street, walked for a while in Indian-file, then, tiring of their escapade, went back to the side where the grass bank verged on the road, and tramping through the swept-up leaves, counted the number of stormwater gratings they passed.

When they reached the photographer's studio they went back up onto the pavement to see if there was anything new going on. The photographer's window was hard to miss because, as Vargas put it, this was the only 'public place' in a street of apartment blocks.

'The photographer bears one of the most personal stamps of our time – the hallmark of specialization.' (This, too, was one of Vargas' formulations.) He specialized exclusively in photographing soldiers. His signboard was the very essence of modernity: it bore just one huge letter P, the first letter of both his name and his profession. P had long since outgrown the times when people strove to capture individual peculiarities – noses, moustaches, grimaces – copulating horses, a traffic policeman knocking off the hat of a passing lady cyclist with his baton, a small dog holding up its leg against a goal-post, the pining bride-groom, head-on collisions, or an absent minded citizen strolling in bright sunshine with his umbrella. P was searching for the synthesis.

This is probably why he chose soldiers as his constant theme. He would look happily round the studio packed with young men all in identical clothes, with identical haircuts; and with an eye sharper than a sergeant's he would spot a button that had not been sewn on but simply held in place with a match-stick at the back. He felt sorry, however, for those soldiers who turned up wearing their own socks instead of the regulation issue – they struck him as being lonely.

According to P, the aim of society and of art was to reduce men to a common denominator. And the ultimate aim of this reduction was – SYNTHESIS.

P was aware that his artistic ambitions could never be satisfied with a ready-made synthesis. So, on Sunday afternoon he invited the soldiers with day-leave passes to sample his Swiss-roll; he served the Swiss-roll on other days as well, if any of the soldiers were able to get free. The Swiss-roll eaters were there to smile. In order to obtain a smile of greater uniformity, P devised a scheme, the essence of which was that the soldiers should tell the same joke in turn. P, meanwhile, looked on excitedly to see how the new uniform expression was shaping up – the 'synthetic look' as he described it in his diary.

Yet P was never satisfied – and this is confirmed by his diary – either with himself or his methods. He was ever trying to add a finishing touch, and this is why he proposed a change in the joke-telling technique as well. He first suggested that, in order for the smile to emerge from the same background, they should start telling the joke with that truly impressive, sadly intelligent, brow-puckered, sky-searching gaze with which all (soldier and civilian alike) stare over the photographer's head, even further if possible – over the very rooftops. In short, that they should begin telling the joke with this expression, and all speak simultaneously. This attempted improvement did not, however, yield the desired result. The joke-telling now took on a canon-like, rather contourless form which, according to the entry in his diary, 'led nowhere'.

P did not have a particularly high opinion of the great cardboard head-in-the-hole frames, but they did – to quote his diary again – represent a 'festive synthesis'. P was not fond of ready-made solutions. This is why on the artillery frame, for instance, in addition to gun-barrels, horses, compasses, shrapnel, laurel wreaths, bullet-traces marked by dotted lines, and a busby, he painted in a chisel and a coffee-cup. Those who put their heads through the holes accepted these two additions as part of the regalia of artillery. And the chisel and coffee-cup were accepted without demur by the photo-admiring members of the family, the brides, the brides' families, female friends (faithful and faithless), and even quite chance viewers, whose trust in the photograph as a depiction of reality was so profound that they did not even notice whether the picture had been taken out of an album or a wallet. Thus – as P recorded – 'a new brush-stroke has successfully been added to the picture of SYNTHESIS.'

Vargas did not perhaps see the problems quite so much from the inside as P. He was just another of the loafing onlookers who get in the way. At any rate, his attention was primarily focused on the cardboard frames. Now, as he entered the studio with Lawrence, and saw P feeding his guests with Swiss-roll through the head-holes in the frame, a thought which had been troubling him for some time began to formulate itself more fully, so he immediately called up Helmuth on the walkie-talkie:

'Reality is in fact a permanent frame: it is only the men moving behind it that change.'

They were still in the photographer's studio when, for the first time since they had set out, Strezovski called up. (He was trying to contact Lawrence. Three times he repeated his own name, then his nickname, then Lawrence's name, and finally his nickname: Corky.)

'Some people are just incredibly irresponsible,' Strezovski could be heard complaining, 'you can talk to them till you're blue in the face.' (Lawrence now turned up the volume and hung the walkie-talkie on the fairly low-hanging chandelier by looping the leather strap round the bulb of one of the crystal candles. This he did in the belief that Strezovski was now going to make some kind of pronouncement which it would be a pity not to listen to as a lecture for merely formal reasons, provided of course it was of satisfactory quality and the audience was available.)

'This boy in the neighbouring yard,' the voice could be heard more strongly now from under the chandelier, 'the one I've already told you about, and if you remember I did not fail to point out that he may be an excellent artisan and altogether a constructive man but I saw him setting off for work around eleven o'clock this morning. Not that this would be so terrible on its own. I mean, I have no bones to pick with him and, who knows, he may have been meaning to work late in the afternoon. I don't know, so I'm not able to judge. But what do you think I saw when I was looking! He lit his welding-torch, let it burn for a while, then went over to some kind of tin washbasin. Well, even that's not too bad. But hardly has he started to fool about with this basin than he spots this bit of skirt passing the open gate; I've told you about the little slut before as well. And what does he do?! Leaves his welding-torch burning, rushes out into the street and starts messing about with her right there.'

'And what training did he have?' Lawrence interjected, going up to the chandelier and putting his question in neutral tones, though somewhat theatrically all the same.

'What training! That's the best part of it. Just listen – you'll die with laughing when I tell you.' (Hearty laughter burst out, not only from above the chandelier but also from behind the cardboard frames.) 'A graduate water-pipe installer! A graduate water-pipe installer! At least, that's how he describes it. I ask you! I mean, I've heard of graduate chemists or graduate engineers, but a graduate water-pipe installer? ... Don't tell me they give degrees in that now! ...'

Everyone laughed. Lawrence looked round the room and nodded at everyone, smiling to show that this was precisely the response he had expected.

They did not recover their composure until P had clambered up onto a small desk, less than one square metre in size, and approached the chandelier. He held his back straight and bent his knees slightly forward, half-crouching, so that his face was level with the walkie-talkie.

'Please do not resent,' he began, 'this intrusion into the programme on the part of a perfect stranger. I am P, and I know that I speak both for my guests and myself when I say that this was an excellent story. I should like, however, to take the liberty of asking whether the young artisan in question had previously worked anywhere else and, if so, how he had behaved.'

After asking his question, P drew back from the chandelier.

The answer was not short in coming.

'An excellent question! I was hoping that somebody would ask this ... Indeed he had worked elsewhere. He had been half way round the world. He'd been to Germany, he'd been to Denmark, even to Holland. But he wasn't happy, he said, because he didn't know the languages. Now do you really think this is why he wasn't happy? Like hell! People who don't do their work properly can never be happy ... He left his welding-torch – burning! ... Just to chitter-chatter! ... God knows when he stopped chatting her up ... And meanwhile his torch was burning ...'

Lawrence and Vargas did not attribute any special significance to this tale, and neither of them mentioned it on the way down to the river. About 30 metres after leaving

P's studio they turned into the long street which leads straight down to the boats. As far as the first corner, the pavement was tarred and so was the road; after that 'civilization abruptly ended', as Vargas liked to say. On the right side of the street there was just a half-metre wide red brick pavement, while the open ground between the pavement and the road was dusty, rutted, and overgrown in places with weeds. The weeds were especially thick directly in front of the tarred part of the road, and in places even covered the tar. Anyone who had only recently arrived in the town would have thought that at one time the whole street had been properly tarred but that it had gradually managed to strip off this cover.

In the shallow ditch beside the pavement, Lawrence came across a worn-out hat – which might have easily been lying for days in the river before the kids had kicked it up this far – and fished it out from among the potato-peels with a stick, on the end of which he managed to twirl it before flinging it about 15 metres away. He suggested to Vargas that they should play rounders with it, but Vargas could not find a suitable stick. He thought of asking Lawrence to lend him his three-legged hunting-stool, but on the one hand it would have been too short and thick and on the other Lawrence would probably not have been too happy to let him have it.

They continued on their way towards the river.

Lawrence again took up the threads of the conversation. 'Some people in the office think,' he began, 'some people think ...'

'Who?' Vargas interrupted, being still in a philosophical vein and feeling, after the inspiration derived from the speech to the cardboard frames, that he was now getting closer, closer than ever, to the great truths of life. 'Who? Who and how many support the assertions of which you are about to tell me? And on the basis of what opinion polls was it established that these opinions had arisen? Was it ascertained what the motives were of those who conducted the polls, and of those who subscribed to these opinions?'

'You have raised a most valid point,' Lawrence conceded. He had, in the meantime, just rediscovered the hat he had flipped away a short while ago, and was prodding it with his stick. 'Indeed, you are to some extent completely right, because one of our fundamental aims is truth and knowledge. I myself am not one to believe in any kind of reliance on subjective manipulation. In my opinion, moreover, the conflict is somewhat contrived and hence does not reveal but rather conceals the true contradictions. In all likelihood, we could establish the requirement that the phenomena should be referred to after indicating their sources, or even in the final count exclusively through their sources, but would we not thereby deny the relative independence of the phenomenon? The dialectic of action and reaction? And, most important, by contrasting the most detailed specification of these sources and the disregard of this specification, we divert our attention towards a false dilemma instead of concerning ourselves with the phenomena *per se*, instead of concentrating on the true contradictions between positive and negative phenomena and persevering in our struggle against negative phenomena. We must beware of directing our weaponry against anti-thesical, imaginary paper-tigers, while behind our backs the real danger continues to lurk.'

Vargas felt that they were now getting down to the nitty-gritty, and did not want to find himself taking the back seat either in show of brilliance or display of erudition. He kicked the hat further on, then replied:

'I agree absolutely with what you say. There is, however, something I should like to put straight: a scientific approach and a spirit of veracity alone are not enough; we must still beware of forcing true contradistinctions into a cul-de-sac, of turning our concrete ideas into abstract theses; we must rather direct them towards principles and practice. But could we – I wonder – either in theory or in practice follow the path of Chinese ideology and justifiably call upon the metaphor of the paper tiger to corroborate our contentions?'

'How very right you are,' Lawrence hastened to reply. 'Certainly, we should not have recourse to Chinese ideology and symbolism – though this was not what I in fact had in mind. I do agree with you, all the same, that I might have expressed myself more clearly and that the allusion to the paper-tiger was far from fortunate.'

Vargas merely nodded. They agreed, after this, that their brief exchange of views on the prevailing state of affairs and on the opinions of people at the office had been most useful. It occurred to Vargas, as an afterthought, that they had not been strictly accurate in their analogy, because the paper-tiger was not so much the symbol of China as of American militarism described in terms of a Chinese metaphor. But they promptly decided that this trifling side-issue could make little or no appreciable change in their mutual outlook. Meanwhile, they had reached the river bank.

Here they met up with their customary companions. And with the customary clash of interests (card-players vs. football-players, fishers vs. swimmers). There too was the tall, lean, 60-year-oldish woman in black whose attempts to organise a choir repeatedly misfired. Aunt Lizzy was also there – true to her custom – firmly facing towards the opposite bank, in the direction of the Holy Office, opening and closing her mouth every few seconds. The water in front of her was fairly deep, the bank sandy. This was the favourite spot of the tag-players, who prided themselves on being able to lip-read Aunt Lizzy. Some of them discovered that by swimming close up to the bank they could hear her as well. At any rate, they all agreed that the only word she uttered was: TOOOOO-NY, with a long drawn-out O. What nobody noticed, however, was that Aunt Lizzy also had her eye on them, and even joined in their little game: her OOOOO lasting exactly as long as one of the young men could stay underwater.

This afternoon, there was quite a crowd at the river. Three separate teams were playing around in front of Aunt Lizzy; and on the opposite bank, the landing-stage (a narrow wooden platform jutting out about 10 metres above the water) was jam-packed with divers. The water at the far end of the landing-stage was really quite deep, and with a single plunge it was possible to dive through the luke-warm surface water to the cooler layers beyond without making a stroke. It was one of those days when all agreed that the water was great, not so much on account of the temperature – for, as has already been mentioned, the surface, was even a little warmer than one would have ideally liked – but rather because of its caressing softness which cushioned our strokes and quietened them down. Even after someone had dived, there was no spurt of white spray, just a shower of heavy drops which rose up and then fell lazily back. A little higher up, by the bend, where the bank narrows to a strip between the river and the houses, not the slightest ripple could be seen on the water.

Next to the landing-stage, two rowing-boats were moored. These were used for going across to fetch visitors who called across from the other bank. One of the boats belonged to the Holy Office, the other to the owner of a vineyard. For the Holy Office one had to shout HELLO TOOONY, and for the owner of the vineyard, HELLO ESTIII. At some time the boatman for the Holy Office had been called Tony. Before crossing, Tony used to draw the boat up towards the bank, then run right to the end of the landing-stage and leap off into the boat, the momentum being sufficient to carry him to the other side without rowing a stroke. He used the oars only for steering, drawing the swirling water with both arms towards the bow to guide the boat in the opposite direction.

But Tony had long since left the Holy Office, though his name had remained, symbolically perhaps, on the bank. The new boatman was rather hard of hearing: often one had to shout for him for a good half hour. Those whose visits were more frequent had been known, in their impatience, to change their cry to HELLO ESTIIII because they now knew the vineyard owner. But even this tactic was not always successful because the shouting could not be heard from the vineyard, where often the whole family was working. When this happened, everyone around would join in the shouting, the card-players first and the fishermen last. Suddenly, the lady in black would appear (she was never seen coming), whose voice was the sharpest and most penetrating on the whole river-bank. She would draw up the shouters in a semicircle, imposing upon them her never-once-disputed authority. Only Aunt Lizzy would stay where she was, thus leaving room to conjecture whether her position represented a stage in the transition from the age of chorus to the age of drama or rather an eccentric gesture of individuality belonging to pre-chorus-age patterns of communication.

The answer to this conjecture was generally expected to be furnished by the boat's arrival, an answer which though not fully comprehensible would – so most of them felt at least – reveal that time tended rather to advance towards Aunt Lizzy than to recede from her. Although the arrival of each boat represented to a large extent a personal success for the lady in black, she was never able to keep her chorus intact once the boat had actually arrived. Nor was it of any avail for the lady in black to explain to them the meaning of art and plead with them to stay together for art's sake, when the majority objected that the continuance of the chorus would be utterly pointless since the boat was already there.

This time, the shouting did not last even a quarter of an hour. In the case of Horváth, Strezovski, and Mrs Helmuth, who had arrived at the bank somewhat later, it did not last even that long. The chorus was still trying out the TOOONY variant, without having switched over for even a second to the HALLO ESTIIII. A young engineer from the office – Theo Butor – came across for them; he was a keen oarsman, who was quick to seize such opportunities of getting in ahead of the regular boatmen. Theo liked to launch himself off by running to the end of the landing-stage. But now, because of the bathers, this was impossible. So he just shoved himself off the bank with an oar and propelled himself across with long powerful strokes. When he was about 20 metres from the bank he began to smile, and the disbanding chorus smiled back. The journey to the bank, however, proved to be fairly long, so engineer Butor thought it advisable to greet them while still on his way. This morale-boosting gesture was joyfully reciprocated by those waiting on the bank.

Theo Butor was a most promising student at the Technical College. He was one of those who were interested in the shape of buildings to come and who conceived the design of the future more or less as a LONG THING WITH A BIG TALL ONE AT THE END. Today, of course – five or six years after his graduation – Theo realised that this had been a hopelessly naïve conception, inspired by his limited personal experience. Nowadays of course he, and the majority of his colleagues as well, preferred to define the future of architecture as GROWING INCREASINGLY COMPLEX.

A rough stone path led to the Holy Office. The premises were situated in what had once been a privately-owned villa. Theo conducted the visitors right through the acoustics department, the office of the research team engaged on the technology of manna-storage, the electronic church-bells department, and the tower-planning rooms. Then they arrived at the office of the red-haired director – a truly spacious room designed to accommodate not only his negotiating team but also the public.

On one side of the longish table sat the red-haired director and the negotiating team, and on the other sat Weidelberger, the Archdeacon, and his colleagues. Lawrence, Strezovski, Horváth, Vargas, Mrs Helmuth and Theo Butor took their places on a small podium running along the wall, railed in rather like a balcony. Theo immediately ordered five coffees, plus one without sugar for himself.

'DrDrDr Weidelberger,' the red-haired director began with (apparently) a stutter. 'Dear DrDrDr Weidelberger, I should like to express our unbounded gratitude, Doctor Doctor Doctor Weidelberger, for your invaluable comments, which have been of such immense assistance to us in the preparation of the plans.'

(Some of the monks were already beginning to chuckle – and the red-haired director's colleagues and those sitting on the podium were also beginning to laugh – at the director's over-earnest introduction, which left no-one in any doubt that the Archdeacon possessed three doctorates. The red-haired director, however, was either oblivious of their reaction or simply intent on ignoring it. At all events, he continued with his speech.)

'My devoted and capable colleagues have in fact solved the problem of the statics of the downward-pointing tower. We are, nevertheless, deeply indebted to you, DrDrDr Weidelberger, for your precious reminder that the church should in the first instance be an architectural symbol, the symbol of an age-old tradition, the conservation of which is a pressing imperative. Needless to say, we promptly set about the task of conservation, endeavouring to remain true to the upstriving verticals so expressive of the yearning for eternal truth, and at the same time to preserve the somewhat crude vigour and expressive force of the original materials – wood and stone. (The red-haired director looked around with satisfaction at this point, made a short impressive break, then continued.) Nor however did we fail to pay the most profound – I might almost say religious – respect, he added with a smile, to those fundamental ideas, retaining them and enriching them with the freshest fruits of our research, and thus, I may claim, rendering the constructions themselves more commodious. And now, consider these plans, dear Doctor Doctor Doctor (sniggering once again broke out from several parts of the room), for as you yourself are well aware, ours is the only architect's office to specialise in these problems. Let us get right down to brass tacks straight away,' said the director – raising himself in his seat and raising his voice, too, to a shout – 'let us begin with the Consecrated Water. Over the past few centuries there have been – have there not? – complaints that the use of ordinary marble-fonts is not sufficiently hygienic, and many have been distressed by the fact that their index fingers remain wet after making the sign of the cross. Simply to dry them would have been disrespectful and irreverent, yet to leave them wet was disagreeable. Now' – and at this juncture the director rose to his feet – 'our Office has resolved this age-old dilemma. Yes! The marble font has, naturally, been left in its customary place, though of course there is no longer any water in it; it has instead been covered with a special sponge resembling a wooden board. When the members of the congregation reach out over the font, an old-fashioned funnel, which is caused to emerge by the operation of a photo-electric cell, appears above their hands, permitting a few drops of consecrated water to fall upon their fingers, any excess water being soaked up by the subjacent sponge. And that's not all! In this space of but a few square metres in which the sign of the cross is made, the respective member of the congregation in concluding the action makes a rightward movement of the hand thus causing a delicate circulation of the air which, I am so bold as to claim, precipitates a unique and wonderful thermochemical process which has the effect of causing the superfluous consecrated water and any chance traces of perspiration to vanish unremarked from the hand of the said member of the congregation.'

(The red-haired director resumed his seat. Then when his colleagues, followed by the members of the gallery and some of the monks, began to clap he stood up again and joined them in prolonged applause.)

Once the clapping had begun to die down, Strezovski stood up.

'Kindly permit me,' he shouted through the still vibrant applause, 'permit me – although an uninvited participant in the negotiations, to relate a story which, I believe, may be instructive to all of us.'

All turned towards him, and Strezovski continued:

'Some people are just incredibly irresponsible. You can talk to them till you're blue in the face. Take this boy from the yard next door, for instance – the one I've already told you about, and if you remember I did not fail to point out that he may be an excellent artisan and altogether a constructive man, but I saw him setting off for work around eleven o'clock this morning. Not that this would be so terrible on its own. I mean, I have no bones to pick with him and, who knows, he may have been meaning to work late in the afternoon. I don't know, so I'm not in a position to judge. But what do you think I saw when I was looking! He lit his welding-torch, let it burn for a while, then went over to some kind of tin washbasin. Well, even that's not too bad. But hardly had he started to fool about with this basin than he spotted this bit of skirt passing the gate – I've told you about the little slut before as well. And what does he do?! Leaves his welding-torch burning, rushes out into the street and starts messing about with her right there.'

'And what training did he have?' Horváth, who was sitting next to him, interjected, putting his question in neutral tones, though somewhat theatrically all the same.

'What training? That's the best part of it. Just listen – you'll die with laughing when I tell you.' (Hearty laughter burst out, not just from above the gallery but also from behind the conference-table.) 'A graduate water-pipe installer! A graduate water-pipe installer! At least that's what he says. I ask you! I mean, I've heard of graduate chemists or graduate engineers – but a graduate water-pipe installer? ... Don't tell me they give degrees in that now! ...'

Everyone laughed. Horváth looked round the room and nodded at everyone, smiling to show that this was precisely the response he had expected.

They did not recover their composure until the Archdeacon, with his back straight as a ramrod, turned somewhat stiffly to Strezovski:

'Please do not resent this intrusion on the part of a total stranger, who wishes to take up the threads of your discourse. I am Archdeacon Weidelberger, and I speak both for myself and my colleagues when I say that this was an excellent story. May I take the liberty of asking, however, whether the young artisan in question had previously worked anywhere else, and, if so, how he behaved?'

After asking his question, the Archdeacon turned round and sat down. The answer was already on its way:

'An excellent question! I was hoping that somebody would ask me this ... Indeed he had worked elsewhere. He had been half way round the world. He'd been to Germany, he'd been to Denmark, even Holland. But he wasn't happy, he said, because he didn't know the languages. Now do you really think this is why he wasn't happy? Like hell! People who don't do their work properly can never be happy ... He left his welding-torch – burning! ... Just to chitter-chatter! ... God knows when he stopped chatting her up, the little slut. And meanwhile his welding-torch was burning ...'

Most of them nodded towards Strezovski, then the red-haired director took over the meeting again:

'I fully agree with all that the previous speaker, my friend Strezovski has said. Cases such as this do exist. And it's a good thing to know about them. Permit me, however, modestly to continue with our fruitful discussion by outlining what has been further proposed by the industrious workers of our firm in order to bring about the construction of as perfect a cathedral as possible through our joint efforts. Have I, I wonder, already mentioned our special device for illuminating the Bible? The congregation, seated in their pews, open the Bible placed in readiness before them: when they do so, light pours forth, activated, naturally, by a photosensitive cell. But what kind of light – if you will permit me Doctor Doctor Doctor Weidelberger to claim your attention – what kind of light? The photosensitive cells react to the movement of the head, and two beams run along parallel with the reader's eyes to the end of the line. But wait: I have not yet told you what kind of light this is! Our chemists and opticians have succeeded in developing a shade of light identical to the colour of the parchment used in ancient Rome by the hounded and persecuted Christians! Behold – here we have the most perfect synthesis of classic tradition and the very latest techniques!...'

(Applause again greeted his words, the only difference being that this time the red-haired director remained standing and joined in the clapping from the very start.)

'And that is still not all,' he continued, after allowing brief pause at the end of the clapping, 'not all, by any means. I still have not told you of our solution to the acoustic problem, which – and I doubt that you would ever have guessed it – is based simply on perforated bricks. Miraculous and simple. I might say, holy and simple. Nor have I mentioned our air-conditioning system, which produces temperatures varying to suit the respective age of the members of the congregation – this being determined by a carbon test of their teeth. The apparatus is, of course, equipped with a regulator which reacts to artificial teeth.'

'Most interesting, indeed,' said the Archdeacon. 'And for my own part I should like to assure you that I completely share the ideas, conceptions and theories thus far expressed. Now, alas, duty calls, and I therefore propose that we continue this fruitful exchange of views tomorrow afternoon.'

The Archdeacon then asked Lawrence for the loan of his walkie-talkie, apologising for his absent-mindedness by explaining that both his sets had been left behind in the boat and that this was why he was obliged to turn to Lawrence for help. Lawrence readily handed him the machine.

'Manna four? ... Manna four? ... Manna two, here ... You can unmoor the boats. We'll be down in three minutes ...'

The Dean returned the walkie-talkies with thanks. Everyone shook hands with everyone else (including the observers), then, accompanied by the bowing director, the monks left the hall.

Lawrence, Vargas, Strezovski, Horváth and Mrs Helmuth next went to call upon some people they knew in the Holy Office. (Vargas noted to himself that none of the grey walls had quite caught the right shade of mouse-grey.) Everyone was commenting on the Archdeacon's visit and on the way the negotiations had gone. The general feeling was that the discussions were moving in the right direction. They did, however, find the director's way of stressing the Archdeacon's academic status both strange and somewhat ridiculous. The overwhelming majority considered Theo Butor's unbiased comment as reflective of their own sentiments:

'It would have been quite enough to say doctor just once.'

FOURTH INTERMEZZO

(About the most important)

That day, Granasztói was elected a member of the Board of the Institute. After the meeting, everyone shook hands with Granasztói. His closest friends, including Kavanomoku, also kissed him on both cheeks, while others settled for an in-between expedient – shaking his hand and draping a congratulatory left arm over his shoulder. In delivering his good wishes, Tilden added 'And now? ...' to indicate that he expected Granasztói to live up to his position in this new sphere of activity.

(Tilden, in fact, had proposed that Granasztói be elected the new member of the Board, after declaring that the Board of the Institute had been performing invaluable work during the past period, although progress had been marred by some slight deficiencies. 'I should like to impress upon you,' Tilden had declared, 'the need for devoting especial attention to the emergent problems. And it is in this sphere, I feel, that we shall require the dedicated efforts of the members of our Board.')

There was in the atmosphere an air of festivity, mingled with a touch of intimacy. As soon as the meeting was over, Mrs Kanelakis immediately opened the windows; and now – while standing around for an unusually long time in irregular groups – they were able to relish the fresh air, which normally they breathed only in the street, wafting right into the room. In this one, now ready for cleaning, a close intimacy was suddenly established, as with neighbours or colleagues whom we have known for a long time and to whom, all of a sudden we start speaking of our own lives.

Granasztói was thinking how human, even lyrical at times, the world of meetings could be. It crossed his mind that, during the long drawn-out debates, when they were simply unable to reach any decision, any conclusion, it was in the end the human factor that triumphed, obliging them imperceptibly to alter their goals and strive with united strength to end the meeting. And gradually – as if through the operation of some secret sorcery – it would suddenly materialise, as the Chairman himself would declare, that the debate had actually been most profitable and fruitful, that it had led somewhere, that it had from its very inception been leading in that direction. At such times one felt like a poet who, while stringing his words together, suddenly and unexpectedly discovers that what lies before him on the paper is already a poem. The graphite-grey window opening onto the whiteness of the Unending.

Sensing that this was no run-of-the-mill occasion, Granasztói invited the present company to take their customary coffee 'and other things' (as he pointedly added) not in Kavanomoku's office but 'for the sake of a change' at the EL ROMINGUEZ restaurant. The invitation was gladly accepted by the majority.

At the EL ROMINGUEZ, the question of *what is the most important?* was raised.

Strezovski and Durrell ordered jointly ('complementarily', as Strezovski explained it), that is, Durrell ordered a pork chop and Strezovski liver with garlic, with a request to the waitress to switch the garlic from the liver to the chop. It may have been precisely this trifling incident that Strezovski had in mind when he found himself thinking: 'It is indeed important that we never restrict ourselves to only one alternative.'

Kavanomoku at once resumed the discussion, not neglecting to point out that the statement he was about to venture might well be considered heretical; then he declared tersely:

'DISALIENATION IS WHAT IS MOST IMPORTANT.'

'That goes without saying,' began Ms Margit, rapping her fork on her plate to create a corridor of sound along which her words might travel. 'It goes without saying. But we must not lose sight of the importance of the projection of the *ego*. The subjective ego must be projected outwards so that it can find its place in objective reality.'

'For in reality the work of art,' said Dr Weidelberger, taking up the thought, 'is none other than the subjective reflection of objective truth.'

'I'm sure we all agree on these points,' said Kismarton tentatively, 'only I think – this is sort of my personal opinion – that it isn't great philosophy that's the most important, nor is it how eloquently one is able to conceptualize things. It's that everyone should speak straight from the heart. What I mean is that it's not so much great philosophy that's important, but rather the economic basis and the word that springs from the heart.'

At this point Hartmann arrived and, after indicating to the waitress that he would order later, he asked leave to speak:

'I should just like to say a few brief words about a consideration which has in all probability already been raised but not been given its due attention. To my way of thinking, we should not disregard the fact that the work and the creator should be conceived as a whole. No matter whether we attempt to separate the work from the creator, or the creator from the work, we find ourselves in an impasse. Historically, in their genesis and in their chemical make-up, the two are conjoined. There is no creator without a work, and vice versa. Because ...'

'If I might just put in a word here – please excuse the interruption, but I shan't take a moment – just a very brief word ...' said Kismárton, leaning over the table, '... On every occasion one should be building up, yet at the same time destroying a world. The sensory world, for instance. Retention-disjunction. Do you follow? *Retention-disjunction*! Dialectically – if I have managed to make myself clear.'

'We should, indeed, never lose sight of the dialectic,' replied Hartmann. 'And I say so advisedly, for the creator and the work must constitute a unity. One must stand up against those attitudes which do not recognise the dialectical compromise, but at the same time one must respect the opinions of individuals.'

'It is also important, of course,' Kismárton resumed, 'that in the bloom of youth our sense of wonderment should be fused with our mature knowledge as we hurtle headlong in the electric locomotive of this giddy age.'

'Please do not get me wrong,' said Lyertovsky, raising his voice, 'but I think that basically Kismárton is right, and that the heart *is* at the centre of it all. *The heart.* The hearts of all, and of each and every one of us. No matter whether our view is macro – or microcosmic.'

'There is perhaps a way of bringing these viewpoints closer together,' Kavanomoku interrupted, passing his glass across the table to be filled by Durrell. 'We could try to establish that in the matter of art not only objective but also subjective relations are important, because only through recognition of their mutual interdependence can the route towards disalienation be revealed.' After these words, Kavanomoku half drained his 0.10 litre glass (it was he who had made the decision when the waitress had asked whether she should bring these or larger glasses for the wine and soda), and then drew the attention of the assembled company to the fact that 'the man of the day had not yet had a chance to speak.'

'I, for one,' Granasztói began, 'did not really mean to take part in the discussion. It was not my intention to speak, so what I'm going to say is purely my own personal opinion, because I'm now speaking simply in my own name. It is my personal opinion – and others perhaps will agree with me here – that the most important step has now been taken by entering into a serious analytical examination of the subject under consideration, i.e. what constitutes the most important. I feel that this is the most important, both in art and in general.

This met with full agreement.

Kavanomoku ordered the next bottles of wine and soda-water, cautioning the waitress to bring the 'seltzer' in blue bottles, because if you use soda-water from white bottles it looks simply as if you're watering the wine. Green bottles would also do.

ILDI'S PORTRAIT IN SALICYL

Scattone was the first to wake. But when, hardly a metre from his feet, sitting on a chair in front of the bedstead, he saw the woman in black (whom he was accustomed to meeting on the river bank), he was convinced that he must still be dreaming and so he went back to sleep. An hour later he woke again, at about the same time as Rogers. The woman in black was still sitting there, bolt upright, her right hand outstretched, reposing on her umbrella as on a royal sceptre. Rogers had not yet noticed anything, and was busy trying to get music from the radio on the bedside table between the beds. Finally, as he was attempting to stand up in the half-metre space between the beds (he always got out of bed on the right foot) he caught sight of the old woman in the three-winged mirror with the dirty green frame to the right of Scattone's bed. Rogers sank back. Now they both knew.

The old woman stretched out towards the blind with her umbrella, wound the cord round the metal prong, and jerked. The blind shot up. In the sudden inrush of brightness the black specks on her face stood out sharply from the surrounding wrinkles. Light stripes and circles played over her black dress. She was like a mosaic in coal. (Rogers did not consider it impossible that she had some connection with the coal which had been dumped on the pavement in front of their building). If one were to pour water on her, she might easily shrivel up. Since the day before yesterday, however, there had been no water in this part of the town. (This may have influenced the timing of her visit). A soda-water bottle might have done just as well, but they were not able to go down and fetch one. The old woman was sitting on their trousers. All life-lines between themselves and expedient action had been severed: the Coal Mosaic had become Mistress of Motion. Rogers and Scattone looked out from under the blankets as she teased the cord of the blind with her umbrella, then stood up to see if the decoration on the ceiling was a fresco or just an ordinary picture that had been stuck there. After prodding it with the tip of her umbrella, she sat down again on their trousers.

The rumbling of trams could be heard from the street and, at fairly regular intervals, the cursing of passers-by as they were brought up short by the heap of coal on the pavement (many even stumbled over it as well). Then the old woman was heard to utter. Her voice had a rather nasal tone, and she spoke without gesture or expression. As soon as the last sound had ceased (or even before she would clamp her jaws together so that no trace of what had been said should remain for even the briefest instant. Her expression was exactly as it had been before she spoke. Next to her was the window, with the curtain cord still swinging lightly in front of it; behind her the cupboard, on top of which was a precarious pile of papers; to her right, in front of Roger's bed, the writing-desk, and on the desk-lamp a paper busby. Nothing had changed. Scattone and Rogers were no longer quite sure that the question really had been asked ('WHERE ARE THE MINUTES-BOOKS?'), so that their silence constituted less a stubborn refusal to reply than an adjustment to the continuing and increasingly convincing state of changelessness.

The question was repeated twice (at five second intervals, and in exactly the same way as on the first occasion). There could now no longer be any doubt that it had been uttered, though it had produced only the very slightest vibration which charged the air with a shortlived tension, only to be dissipated a few moments later as the tiny sound-ripples subsided and were smoothed away, like the coal-dust stirred up on the street by passing feet. Rogers and Scattone were aware that the status quo might be maintained without any special difficulty right up till lunch-time, possibly even longer. But by then, hopefully, something would have happened to tip the balance in their favour.

This, indeed, might easily have been the case if the unexpected had not come to the old lady's aid. It might have seemed, perhaps, that the pile of papers stacked on top of the cupboard and flopping over the edge in places had never been so securely positioned as in this present state of perfect equilibrium. It would appear, however, that the danger was building up in direct proportion to the tenuous balance that was now on the point of perfection. Now that a static harmony had been achieved between the room itself, the protagonists of the action, and the chance impulses penetrating through from the world beyond, the knife-edge balance could be righted no further and (though those present were unaware of the fact) everything was teetering on the brink of collapse. In such a situation, then, it was perfectly logical that the stacks of paper should topple over, most of them landing on the floor beside the Coal Mosaic. Amongst these papers were the Minutes-Books.

When the old woman bent down to retrieve them it seemed as though several of her upper joints were breaking. Nevertheless, she calmly picked up the bundles and some of the loose papers, set aside what was of no interest to her, spread out the material she had retained in her lap and then, without raising her eyes, began to read in her habitual way:

First Minutes-Book

Present: Scattone, Rogers, Strezovski, Yomtobian, Arak, Eftehari and Sziveri
The meeting began at: 20.00, ended at: 24.35 (00.35)
Agenda: a) Administrative matters
        b) Miscellaneous

under a) *Scattone*: (after welcoming those present) To begin with, I think I truly express the sentiments of all present when I state that we are ready to collaborate and co-operate with all other organisations, institutions, or even individuals engaged in activities similar to our own. Collaboration undoubtedly contributes towards enabling us to accelerate our further growth and gain an understanding of our respective problems by 'learning from one another's errors', if I may put it this way. We do not envisage any kind of cliqueishness whatsoever; we will glady advance arm-in-arm with anyone, happily adopt new outlooks and fresh initiatives, and willingly share the fruits of our joint endeavours.

Yomtobian: All this collaboration and so on is all very well. I am all for it. Indeed, this is the right road to follow. My only reservation is that I am not sure it can be done, because in order to collaborate with these various bodies and organs, we would need to be something ourselves. And we – if I may so so – are nothing. We are not even so much as a commission, or even a committee. We are merely accustomed to meeting here at your place because it doesn't matter if we talk at the tops of our voices. Sometimes, if one of us happens to be flush, we get together in a café to let off steam. But that's not a commission – it's nothing.

Rogers: I couldn't agree more with what has just been said. We do, indeed, need to be modest. Without modesty we cannot presume to perform worthwhile work. (Interjection: What kind of work? – But Rogers continues.) We should not, however, let ourselves become bogged down in formalism. Action does not derive from one's status: on the contrary, status derives from one's action! If we act first, our appropriate organisational form will follow. In my opinion, we should not allow ourselves to be paralysed by the lack of an organisational form. Action does not derive from status, but status from action!

Yomtobian: O.K., O.K., I just said ...

Arak: And in my opinion we shouldn't be dithering over all this action and collaboration. Let's get to work – right away!

Scattone, Rogers, and Eftehari: Hear, hear!

Szigeri: I fully agree with the majority. Surely we do not need to wait around for ready-made solutions and magic forms. But still ... still, it would be different if we were at least some kind of committee. It would be easier to set about forging the links. Our problem is that we're just a little too private. Though perhaps privatisation ...

Eftehari: Yes, but can we just arbitrarily form a committee like this without at least holding prior consultations?

Arak: Well, how about setting up an Interim Committee?

All present approved this proposal and decisively and unanimously declared that an *interim committee* should be constituted.

under b) Those present noted that the following meeting of the INTERIM COMMITTEE was scheduled for 10 November at 19.00 – at the regular venue.

obliged to send written notification of this without fail to everyone else concerned (i.e. to everyone except themselves), thus ensuring the democratisation of initiative and interimmediacy, and avoiding the perils of unilateral control.

At the following meeting, the first item on the agenda would be TO DETERMINE WHAT WAS THE BEST TIME. Other points on the agenda would include the question of collaboration and miscellanea.

Scattone m.p.

After she had finished reading the First Minutes-Book, the old woman looked up for a moment. Rogers and Scattone lay silent and helpless on the bed.

The old woman continued.

Second Minutes-Book

Present: Scattone, Rogers, Strezovski, Yomtobian, Arak, Eftehari and Sziveri

The meeting began at: 19.30, ended at: 03.10
Agenda; a) To determine what was the best time
b) Miscellaneous

under a) *Eftehari*: The best time was when we ate the Flying
Bird which Aunt Kathy sent from Sydney. She sent a whole
load of tins – because she had heard that the grub was lousy
here – mostly tinned shrimps. Just with this one tin we
couldn't work out what was inside; all that was written on
the side was Flying Bird. We called everyone along for the
ceremonial opening, but it turned out that the Flying Bird
was some bloody sauce. After that we spent a long time
trying to work out a letter to send to Aunt Kathy which
would touch her soft spot and make her send more parcels.
It was Scattone's idea that the letter should begin like this:
Dear Aunt Kathy, We are most grateful for the first parcel
… But we never got round to writing it in the end.
Yomtobian: That was also a good time when old Péter fell off
his chair. Him, of all people, who never put a foot wrong,
never wasted a single movement, just sat there at the desk
with his hat right in place on the left hand corner. Sziveri
was so shattered he stuffed the chalk into his pocket, but his
eyes were bulging out so much you'd have thought he'd
swallowed it. And he kept burbling: 'Hopp-hopp-hopp, Sir,
hopp-hopp-hopp, Sir,' even when old Péter was back on his
chair again …
Strezovski: But it was even better when that boy from the
next-door yard – the one I've already told you about, and, if
you remember, I did not fail to point out that he may be an
excellent artisan and altogether a constructive man, but I
saw him setting off for work about eleven o'clock one
morning. Not that this would be so terrible on its own. I
mean, I have no bones to pick with him, and, who knows,
he may have been meaning to work late in the afternoon. I
don't know, so I'm not able to judge. But what do you think
I saw when I started looking! He lit his welding-torch, let it
burn for a while, then went over to some kind of tin
washbasin. Well, even that's not too bad. But no sooner has

he started to fool about with this basin than he spots this bit of skirt passing the open gate – I've told you about the little slut before as well. And what does he do? Leaves his welding-torch *burning*, rushes out into the street and starts messing about with her right there.

Sziveri: And what training did he have?

Strezovski: What training? That's the best part of it. Just listen – you'll die with laughing when I tell you. A graduate water-pipe installer! A *graduate* water-pipe installer! At least that's what he says. I've heard of graduate chemists or graduate engineers – but a graduate water-pipe installer! Don't tell me they give degrees in that now! ...

Scattone: Had he worked anywhere before? And, if so, how did he behave?

Strezovski: An excellent question! I was hoping that somebody would ask me this. Indeed he had worked elsewhere. He had been half way round the world. He'd been to Germany, he'd been to Denmark, even to Holland. But he wasn't happy, he said, because he didn't know the languages. Now do you really think this is why he wasn't happy? Like hell! People who don't do their work properly can never be happy ... He left his welding-torch – burning! ... Just to chitter-chatter! ... God knows when he stopped chatting her up, the little slut. And meanwhile his welding-torch was burning ...

Rogers: But still the best time was once in winter when there was a coal shortage (*here the old woman began to read more slowly*) and it was so cold here in the room that Scattone had to turn the pages with gloves on and the landladies, who never had a fridge, simply left their butter in our place to stop it from going off. Anyway, that's the kind of life we were living when, one night as I was coming home around midnight, I spotted a great heap of coal on the corner. I quickly grabbed as much of it as I could carry, staggered home with it, up to the second floor, and rang the bell with my forehead. Scattone came to the door. I ought to tell you that he still wore his Wee-Willie-Winkie pyjamas which had no elastic in the trousers, no cord, nothing, because –

as he himself said many times – you only wear pyjamas when you're horizontal, and in this position you aren't subject to the force of gravity, and the absence of gravity will keep your trousers up far better than a belt with a buckle. Anyway, Scattone opened the door just as two of the landladies appeared (both over 70, and one still an old maid). Now, I couldn't hold the coal any longer, so I dumped half of it into Scattone's hands. That was when gravity took over, and one of the landladies shrieked: 'God, how horrid!'

But that's not the end of it. We carted coal until two in the morning, worked up a good sweat, then went to bed leaving the fire to be lit when we woke up. But in the daylight (*and here the old woman began to read still more slowly, even raising her voice slightly*) it turned out that it wasn't coal we had brought up but frozen mud with a bit of coal-dust on top. The only good it did was that it warmed us up again when we carried it out that evening under cover of darkness and dropped it off the balcony. (*At this point, the old woman stopped. A strained silence followed. Rogers and Scattone dared not look at each other. Another wad of papers slid off the top of the cupboard, but the old lady did not pick them up. Then she went on with her reading*).

Arak: But it was also great when we went to the flicks with Eftehari. It was a pretty lousy film, but Eftehari seemed to be getting a kick out of it, and when we met Tsu Tao on the way home, he started telling him all about it with great enjoyment. The plot. If only he'd just stuck to the plot! But he kept making up his own story. He told him his own version of the film, even though I was right there with him as a living witness. But the best of it was when Tsu Tao got left behind at the corner because Eftehari was so carried away he couldn't slow down, so all the way home he was telling *me* the story of the film we had seen together, lying his head off and concocting a whole lot of stuff we both knew very well wasn't true.

Scattone: But it was also great when we put Mrs Muka's name down for the Underwater Fishing and Diving

Association (or something like that – the UFDA. The aquanauts). Mrs Muka, who's all boobs and bum: she's a widow from our building who doesn't do anything all day except get up at eight in the morning and worry about whether the Russians are coming. She had only her family name up on the door so that if the Russians or anyone else came who wanted to ransack her flat or rape her they might think there was a man living there. Whenever we came up with a woman she always stood right in the doorway and asked primly if we had come to study. When she got her first invitation from the UFDA she was in such a tizz that she went round to every apartment on all four floors asking people's advice about what to do. Then she went off with all this advice to the UFDA, but when she got there she couldn't remember a word of it, so all she could do was tell them over and over what a chaste life she had been living for the last 55 years.

Sziveri: I still think the best time was when we were listening to the radio and playing cards, and they had just finished the late-night news and said: 'We'll be bringing you the news again at five o'clock tomorrow morning,' and Arak, who was just dealing at that moment, muttered sourly: 'Hell, do they think we're going to hang around that long …!?'

After the above contributions, the members present decided to form a Standing Jury. Members: Scattone, Rogers, Strezovski, Yomtobian, Arak, Eftehari and Sziveri. Following consultations by the Standing Jury an appendix to the Minutes-Book was drawn up which was to be fully incorporated in the Minutes-Book.

Minutes-Book of the Standing Jury

Present: Scattone, Rogers, Strezovski, Yomtobian, Arak, Eftehari and Sziveri.
The meeting began at: 01.30, ended at: 02.30
Agenda: To decide what was the best time

The Standing Jury first submitted for consideration the question of the practicability of judging what was the best time. The majority conceded that Rogers was right in saying that in the Iliad they had even made a competition out of judging which was the best and fairest judgement pronounced on any particular issue. The Standing Jury conceded, however, that Arak was also right in pointing out that nothing could be partially transplanted, not even the tradition of the Ancient Greeks. Arak further explained that the Ancient Greeks had provided per diem allowances both for their theatre spectators and for those who participated in democratic decision-making. After this, the Standing Jury stated that they wished to have it on record that a proposal should be made to the Interim Committee for the introduction of per diem allowances.

The Standing Jury then announced that it was unable to accept Strezovski's contribution as a valid entry to the competition as the speech had been used on a prior occasion; it would, consequently, be disqualified.

The Standing Jury did not succeed in reaching a majority decision as to what was the best time, and so no resolution was passed.

The Standing Jury unanimously elected to record only final decisions in the Minutes-Book, and not full discussions. The present minutes had been drawn up in accordance with this decision.

Eftehari m.p.

under b) Miscellaneous: For the first time, the Interim Committee discussed the standing Jury's proposal, and it was agreed that per diem allowances be introduced.

It was also decided that future Minutes-Books should, in conformity with that of the Standing-Jury, contain only the most essential matters and the decisions reached.

The following meeting of the Interim Committee was scheduled for 12 November at 19.00, at the regular venue.

Notification to be given in the customary way.

Since no definitive decision had been reached, the first item on the agenda would again be to determine what had been the best time. The agenda would also include the question of collaboration and miscellanea.

Scattone m.p.

Rogers and Scattone began to breathe more easily. The menace, they now saw, had not taken on a new form, indeed, it seemed to have melted away. They sat up in bed, propping the pillow up against the bed-stead and leaning against it. The old woman made only the briefest pause, then read on:

Third Minutes-Book

Present: Scattone, Rogers, Strezovski, Yomtobian, Arak, Eftehari and Sziveri
The meeting began at: 19.40, ended at: 02.30
Agenda: a) To decide what was the best time
b) Miscellaneous

under a) *Eftehari*: The best time was when we ate the Flying Bird and didn't write anything in the end.
Yomtobian: It was also great when old Péter fell off his chair.
Strezovski: (announced that he was not prepared to compete any longer).
Rogers: But the best time was still when I thought I had found coal in the street and took it up, and poor old Scattone exposed himself to the two landladies, and the next day it turned out to be just frozen mud.
(The old lady suddenly stopped reading. In this drastically abbreviated form, the story gained a fresh provocativeness. 'That's kitsch!' she exclaimed. 'Kitsch, like all concentrates – like hit-songs and concentrated fruit-juice. And what's more it's utterly shallow and commonplace. There's no build-up. You can't just jump straight to the punch-line. No build-up: result – zero. It's worth about as much as the twaddle you hear from that fairy grandson of mine who teaches philosophy and can't

tell you anything except Hegel says this and Heidegger says that, and the truth of course lies somewhere between the two. Plato says this, Aristotle says that – but we know it's a bit of both and none of either.'

'We only wanted the essential ...' Rogers began, but, sensing that he was only making things worse, gave up. Anyway, the old woman had already butted in on him: 'Essential? What essential! The essential's nothing – eyewash! You're groping around for essentials and reality's staring you up the arse.'

'That wasn't what we meant,' groaned Scattone ...

'What then? Out with it!'

Silence fell. Rogers turned slightly to the right, but the mosaic of the old woman still confronted him from the three-faced mirror.

(After this, the old woman nevertheless continued).

Scattone: But what about the time when we put Mrs Muka down for the UFDA and she went along and kept telling them what a blameless life she had lived.

Arak: It was also great when Eftehari was telling me about the film all the way home and Tsu Tao had been left behind long ago.

Sziveri: I still think the best time was when we were playing cards and listening to the late-night news.

(Kitsch! – growled the old woman)

After listening to these contributions, the members present decided to form a Standing Jury. Members: Scattone, Rogers, Strezovski, Yomtobian, Arak, Eftehari, and Sziveri. Following consultations by the Standing Jury an annexe to the Minutes Book was prepared which constituted an integral part of the said Book.

The Minutes-Book of the Standing Jury

Present: Scattone, Rogers, Strezovski, Yomtobian, Arak, Eftehari and Sziveri

The meeting began at: 01.00, and ended at: 01.30

Agenda: To decide what was the best time.

As the Standing Jury did not succeed in establishing what was the best time, no decision was reached on this question.

Eftehari m.p.

under b) The Interim Committee accepted the Standing Jury's report.

It was decided that per diem allowances could not be continued owing to the fact that we were unable to raise a single allowance.

The Interim Committee unanimously seconded the proposal that the competition be discontinued as it was proving to be inexpedient under present circumstances.

The following meeting of the Interim Committee was scheduled for 19 November, at the regular venue.

Notification in the customary way.

The agenda would deal with miscellaneous questions, including the problematics of collaboration.

Scattone m.p.

'Oh well, might as well go on,' said the old woman, and she continued without a pause.

Fourth Minutes-Book

Present: Scattone, Rogers, Strezovski, Yomtobian, Arak, Eftehari, and Sziveri
The meeting began at: 22.00, and ended at: 01.30
Agenda: Miscellaneous

On account of the landladies' (unwonted) opposition, the meeting was held in the street in front of the Cherry Wholesalers. We took out only the most essential furniture: a small table and a few chairs. On account of the dearth of chairs, the table was also used for sitting on.

For a while, the members present were disturbed by passing pedestrians, but soon the only interruption was that of the trams.

Yomtobian: At this time of night you have the feeling that the tram would pick you up even where there was no stop.

Arak: And at this time the sweat is breaking out through the actors' make-up in the theatre on the market-square.

Scattone: It's November, and it isn't even cold.

Strezovski: From where we're sitting, distance is reduced to five or six meaningless points of light.

Rogers: And now the waves on the Danube are flattening out.

Sziveri: And now, since we're talking of it, one recalls that the afternoon and the evening vanish like stones sinking into tall grass.

Eftehari: The sweat of hurry dries on the street and the night disperses into wisps of straw.

Yomtobian: Happiness, in fact, is cool like the earth.

As the cold was closing in, the Interim Committee decided to adjourn the meeting.

While they were taking in the table and chairs, they decided that the following meeting should be held on 23 November at 17.00.

Notification in the customary way.

The agenda would cover miscellaneous questions, including that of collaboration.

Scattone m.p.

The old woman let this pass without comment, and continued:

Fifth Minutes-Book

Present: Scattone, Rogers, Strezovski, Yomtobian, Arak, Eftehari, and Sziveri
The meeting began at: 17.10, and ended at: 23.30
Agenda: Miscellaneous

'Repose is essentially an onomatopaeic word. It comes from repooooooose. When you're dog-tired and you want a zizz, you need repoooooose. That's the origin of the word.'

'I'll marry anyone who's written me a 9-page letter.'

'Banana-splitting.'

'Mozart's dog must have been called Moby.'

'They only accepted Picasso because it was impossible to claim that everyone is a charlatan. Somebody had to be chosen.'

'The Hollywood Bowl was filled to the brim.'

'You need to do physical jerks.'

'Ask for soda-water in blue bottles, not white, otherwise it looks as if you're watering the wine.'

'Said Pierre.'

(What's this 'Said Pierre?' asked the old woman. Rogers readily replied: 'There was a game they used to play: one person would whistle a snatch of a tune and the others had to guess where it came from. But when the snatches got shorter and shorter, Arak lost his patience and asked where 'Said Pierre' came from. Nobody knew. Then he told them – War and Peace.)

The Interim Committee decided that henceforth it would be pointless to write down the speakers' full names as this only led to unnecessary importance being accorded to the individual. The present minutes, therefore, were recorded in conformity with this decision.

The members of the Interim Committee noted that the following meeting was scheduled for 27 November, again at 17.00, and at the regular venue.

Notification in the customary way.

The agenda would cover miscellaneous questions, including that of examining the openings for collaboration.
Scattone m.p.

Sixth minutes-Book

Present: Scattone, Rogers, Strezovski, Yomtobian, Arak, Eftehari, and Sziveri
The meeting began at: 17.40, and ended at: 23.00
Agenda: Miscellaneous

Ildi's portrait in Salicyl.
Scattone m.p.

'And what's this – Ildi's portrait in Salicyl?' asked the old woman. Neither Rogers nor Scattone, however, was capable of reconstructing the events of 27 November, so no explanation was given.

A lengthy silence now fell, during which the only audible sound was that of the curtain cord tapping from time to time against the window-sill.

Then the old woman spoke again: 'Once I was travelling by plane to see that pansy grandson of mine. Before we took off, the air-hostesses explained what had to be done if we suddenly lost altitude. And one of them even reminded us that it was forbidden to smoke under the oxygen mask – "Which would be hard enough, anyway," I said to my neighbour. "Like bloody hell," said my neighbour, an elderly man who never stopped eating chocolate. "Like bloody hell. It takes all sorts ... I had a friend, for instance, who used to smoke in the shower ..."'

MAN'S GREATEST ENEMY

Professor Axelrod made no fuss about the blackboard not having been cleaned. Before making an incisive gesture to cut short the frayed ends of conversations still under way in parts of the room, and before drawing the loose strands of attention more tightly towards him, he picked up the sponge from the table and took it over to the tap. He held off this small tirumph with the self-assurance of a chess player who prefers not to pounce at once on a helpless pawn, or one of those guests who calmly puts on his hat and adjusts his scarf before turning to take his coat from the host or waiter or cloakroom-attendant holding it for him.

The following words, written in the hand of Sharlin (the girl who always wore a turquoise pullover because she thought it went well with mouse-grey), still stood on the blackboard from the previous lesson:

If ours	*If theirs*
BENDING-OVER-BACKWARDS	SLIPPERY CUSTOMERS
SCRUPULOUSLY CORRECT	FORMALLY CORRECT
DISCERNING	DOGMATIC
TO THE POINT	CURT (BRUSQUE)
TRUE TO PRINCIPLES	BIGOTED
NOT ETERNALLY PUTTING THINGS OFF	IN NO HURRY TO GET THINGS DONE

EAGER	GO-GETTING
THEORETICALLY	
SOUND	ABSTRACT
ANTI-DISCRIMINATION	PRO-CONFORMITY
METICULOUS	PEDANTIC
EASY-GOING	WISHY-WASHY
ABLE TO MAKE	
LIGHTNING	PRONE TO JUMPING
DECISIONS	TO CONCLUSIONS

Professor Axelrod, lecturer in the History of World and National Minutes-Books, methodically cleaned the blackboard, then glanced at his watch: he would be starting no more than two minutes late.

'Right,' he began, and paused until the dozen or so students were absolutely quiet. 'Right, then. We may continue with our examination of the Origin of the Minutes-Book. Several decades before the advent of Christianity, as Caius and Hamburger have so nicely observed, 'the revolutionary winds of change had shaken certain deep-rooted values to the foundations.' During this period we may discern two fundamental modes of intervention during discussions: the REFERENTIAL (in which reference is made to the previous speaker) and the NON-REFERENTIAL. Certain persons hold the view that further subdivisions might be possible. For my part, however, I should like to draw your attention only to what is most essential. This distinction is important because it affords us an excellent opportunity to trace the line of development.'

'Initially, the REFERENTIAL intervention came to the fore and proliferated, giving rise inevitably to written records or, more precisely, the keeping of MINUTES-BOOKS, much in the way that the over-issuing of paper money gives rise to inflation, the lack of centralisation to mismanagement, negligence to accidents, dirty hands to disease, or industrious hands to prosperity. Each man is the master of his own fate!

'Let me now attempt to illustrate this with a few examples. Consider, for instance, this case: If a man, X, insists that the market-price of guinea-pigs should be fixed at 52 and not at 62 gulvics, and if, subsequently, another person refers to X's statement, it frequently occurs (and this was particularly true of those times), so, as I was saying, it not infrequently occurs that he neglects to make his intervention in the proper, accepted way: "If I am not mistaken, Mr X would appear to be favouring a *downward* trend in the market-price of guinea-pigs ..." After this nod of acknowledgement to X, one may happily continue one's speech, introducing the counter-arguments. Otherwise, one may gamble on the likelihood that our statement "Surely a high market-price for guinea-pigs would guarantee us equal trading status with Norway?" is sure to provoke from X the reply: "The previous speaker has not, I fear, entirely understood my point."

'Several decades before the advent of Christianity there was an avalanche-like growth, I might say a burgeoning of such diversionary tactics as:

'"I think there may be a misunderstanding here ..."

'"Quite so, though that is not in fact what I said ..."

'"I wonder if we aren't perhaps talking at cross-purposes ..."

'The discussion would then, of course, be pursued in a highly offensive manner, for it was impossible to know what was coming next and where it was all leading. Such diversionary tactics became appreciably more frequent after the second or third meeting on the selfsame question.'

'Then it was' – and at this point professor Axelrod raised his voice to an almost triumphal pitch – 'then it was that the MINUTES-BOOK appeared on the scene! The minutes-book, which, as you are all aware – and as the brothers Grumm have observed – does not primarily serve to put thoughts on record. By its mere existence alone, by its very presence, the minutes-book holds the disputants in check. It does not exist in order to be later read and referred to, but in order to ERADICATE THE BINDWEED FROM THE REFERENTIAL WHEAT-FIELD.

Professor Axelrod was a believer in non-ex-cathedra teaching.

'Ex-cathedra teaching is now an outmoded fashion. Today, in this atomic age of ours, teachers too must be on the move. We can never hope to keep pace with the jet-propelled aircraft if we persist in presenting our material ex-cathedra. No, our approach must be MORE DIRECT.' Unlike most of his colleagues, Axelrod actually had a practical project for stepping out of 'THE MAGIC CHALK CIRCLE OF THE EX-CATHEDRA APPROACH.'

'The cathedra – or lecture-stand – will only cease to be a cathedra once it belongs to everyone!' This was Axelrod's maxim. And, in keeping with his principle, he brought the students up to sit on the lecture-stand during the second half of his class, when the discussion began. ('The time is not far off,' Axelrod declared enthusiastically on several occasions, 'when we will EVEN BEGIN the classes like this.')

In the practical application of his principle, the professor was also aided by the fact that the cathedra was a truly spacious platform, stretching almost from one wall to the other. This enabled him to carry out his maxim to the letter by seating the students in one long row on the platform, from where they gazed with a slight tremor at the rows of empty benches and the door.

Difficulties arose only if – as during this class – more than ten students were present. No matter how closely the chairs were packed (Axelrod's included), only two of the legs of the chairs at either end could be fitted onto the platform.

'The new system has not yet found its centre of gravity. It is still fluid, in a state of flux,' said Axelrod, which is why he procured ceiling hand-straps to enable those seated at either extremity to maintain their balance. A few months of this experience revealed that in the interests of complete uniformity (or DECATHEDRALIZATION, as the professor put it) it would be necessary to install not just two hand-straps but twelve. During the past few days he had been trying to decide whether he should not also make it compulsory for everyone (himself included) to hang onto his strap, thus hastening the destruction of the 'EX-CATHEDRA HOUSE OF CARDS'.

On the present occasion, the burly Livingstone, and Krumov the basketball star, happened to be on the side seats. Apart from these two, professor Axelrod was also making use of the hand-strap. Ms Margit, however, was playing with hers, patting it with a certain feline petulance.

Livingstone, on the left, was the first to ask to speak, holding his free left hand up awkwardly in front of his face.

'Carry on,' said professor Axelrod with a nonchalant smile.

'I should just like to say a word or two in passing on the question of WHAT IS MAN'S GREATEST ENEMY,' Livingstone began.

The row of faces swivelled towards him with interest.

Krumov broke in:

'I couldn't agree more with Livingstone. I should like, however, to ask how we can speak of man's greatest enemy without even mentioning his greatest friends, without at least REFERRING – as the professor said – to them as well. They both, in my opinion, comprise a single dialectical unit.'

'But is it really possible,' asked a young man in rubber galoshes, 'to separate them? Can one isolate, treat on its own, the question of who is man's greatest enemy?'

'Actually, all I meant was ... I mean ... you know,' Livingstone began tentatively.

'Quite so, but it isn't quite as simple as all that,' said Eftehari, entering the discussion at this point. 'Can one speak of man's greatest enemy without even mentioning his greatest friend or at least referring to him? And here I am thinking of the dog. The faithful dog. Can the two problems be separated, or do they form an indivisible whole, such as, for instance, the state and law, production and consumption, export and import, input and output, teacher, and pupil, man and woman, Rosencrantz and

Guildenstern, or Hamlet and Horatio?'

'Or Othello and Iago, perhaps,' the professor added with a satisfied nod.

'Or Little Red Riding Hood and the Wolf?' suggested a voice on the left.

Sharlin, the girl in the turquoise pullover, now came to Livingstone's defence: 'I fully agree with what has been said, but there is a further question I should like to raise: can one simply combine things mechanically in this way? I mean – man's friends and his enemies, high tide and low tide, input and output, and such like. Can one just combine them mechanically? Because it's no good either if ...'

Once again, galoshes spoke:

'At any rate, the truth always lies somewhere between the two. Things can't be separated. But it would also be inadvisable to start making mechanical combinations like this.'

'BUT HOW THEN CAN WE POSSIBLY SPEAK OF ANYTHING AT ALL?!' Livingstone burst out irately.

After this, the even tenor of the debate was somewhat disturbed. The speakers started cutting in on each other, and only fragments of what was said have been preserved in the Pedagogical Minutes-Book:

– because if we are to separate them ...
– combine them, certainly, because otherwise ...
– what about Othello and Iago? ...
– Snow White and the Seven Dwarfs ...
– from a dialectical point of view it seems ...
– combine what is separate? ... cocks here, hens there? ...
– look at the mule, for instance: in terms of formal logic ...
– because on the one hand if we separate, and on the other hand mechanically combine ...
– the shoe and the sock, for example ...
– Desdemona! ...

The long narrow row, headed by the lanky Krumov, tossed back and forth like a Viking ship on the waves until professor Axelrod succeeded in calming the troubled waters with his oily words:

'WHAT WE MUST BEAR IN MIND ABOVE ALL IS MAN ...'

After this the discussion ran far more smoothly. Livingstone once again mentioned that he too considered that the things could not be treated separately, but that he would like to say a word or two in passing about the question of man's greatest enemy, though he was not inclined to doubt for a moment that other attitudes might be possible. Sharlin repeated her warning that the danger of mechanical combination should not be underestimated.

Fresh examples were then produced to substantiate arguments concerning the difficulties inherent in compound or separating.

In the end, however, it was decided that Livingstone should declare what he considered to be man's greatest enemy.

Livingstone replied that, considering the importance of the matter in hand, it might be fitting if he delivered his remarks from the floor. To which Alexrod – with the full approval of the others – responded by drawing attention to the fact that a standing delivery would not be in conformity with the principle of DECATHEDRALISATION, and managed to persuade Livingstone to conclude his speech sitting.

After this, nobody spoke but Livingstone, who lunged twice in quick succession at the hand-strap, then announced:

MAN'S GREATEST ENEMY IS OF COURSE THE SNAKE ...

FIFTH INTERMEZZO

(Respect for tradition)

On this occasion, the company gathered with more than customary enthusiasm at Kavanomoku's office because their host had announced that he would be serving them wine and goodies from his native village.

During this informal get-together they all tucked into the home-made goodies with great gusto and appreciation, and Lawrence did not fail to observe that it is in wine and home-made goodies that the true values are reflected, and what a barbarous act it was to cut down the plane trees on the boulevard leading to the station, and wasn't it dreadful how much time you could waste nowadays trying to find a parking place. To this he added that the significance of tradition should not be undervalued.

All expressed their agreement with him.

Hartmann made a particular point of stressing that he was in full and total agreement with the sentiments just expressed, adding that a condition of rootlessness is injurious; in connection with the meeting two days ago of the Coordination Commitee he wished, with all due respect, to mention that Ms Margit's intervention had been sadly devoid of logic.

'I mean, where is the logic in saying that the new office will have to be located in premises of its own when it would be the simplest thing in the world to put the members of the Committee in the offices of the people with whom they most frequently collaborate?' Hartmann wished to know. He then added with a smirk that in such matters Ms Margit was good for nothing but that in other matters she was good

for something, and that he trusted it would not be necessary
to spell out what he had in mind with 'other matters'.

All indicated that it would not be necessary.

Mbwe declared that although it was not his intention to
defend Margitka, he wished to point out that her speech
had nevertheless had a positive effect, because until Ms
Margit had stood up to speak it had looked as though the
meeting were just going to fizzle out, which would have
been both distressing and regrettable considering the
importance of the agenda – one might almost go so far as to
say its festive character – and considering, too, the presence
of the member of the Supreme Coordination Committee
who had been invited to attend.

Lyertovsky announced that he agreed with the previous
speaker, and that things needed to be given their
appropriate form and place, and that the progressive
tradition had to be nurtured.

Kavanomoku then asked to speak. The Turks, he said,
were in fact absolutely right. 'The Turks are right,' he
repeated, 'ALL is not in vain: centuries of experience
cannot just fizzle out, as Mbwe put it, and be thrown on the
junk-heap. From the point of view of modern society, many
of their practices may not be acceptable, but this does not
mean that they were without rhyme or reason. Because it's
one thing if you've got variety, and plenty to choose from,
but it's quite a different kettle of fish if it's always the same
woman day after day, year in year out. No wonder it won't
work.

All present again voiced their agreement.

POOM-BOOM

In both cases the punchline was a loud report. A shot. Or an imitation of shooting produced by the aid of breath-filled cheeks and the vocal chords.

Poom-boom, or boom-boom.

This evocation of firing was in fact somewhat more nuanced, containing an interplay of variants, as did the red marble monument + inscription in the direction of which the shots had sounded. On one side of this small monument, huddled under the marble overhang as if sheltering from the rain, were the figures of an elderly man and an elderly woman, hands twined together, sorrow in their look. Or perhaps remoteness. On the other side of the rectangular slab stood a Virgin-style mother, children in her arms and round her skirts, wearing a far-away look like that of the two old folk. They were back-to-back, separated by only a thin layer of stone.

The inscription: GRIEF AND HOPE. It was almost as though the eyes of the mother, the children, and the old couple had been blacked out by these words: creativity censored by bashfulness, the narrow rim of the inscription drawing a flimsy canopy under the widespread whiteness of the Finnish night. Like the roof of a building, under which people become members of a family or colleagues. Or the light plastic top of a bus-shelter under which people are gathered, arriving from all directions: office workers setting out in the morning, factory workers returning from their late-night shifts, servers coming back from dawn mass, the widow of a dentist who likes travelling by bus, a 29-year-old

Chemistry teacher who had got blind drunk that night for the first time in his life and now kept shaping his lips wetly round unuttered words and wagging his finger until he chanced on the right gesture to emphasise what he wanted to get across, then uttered a shhhh to his swaggering, far more experienced, boozing-companion who was making a great show of offering non-existent wares to the waiting queuers (Oatmeal bread – try some! Pumpkin bread – buy some! Rinso for those stubborn stains! Rhino horn keeps your tool in trim! Powdered rhino horn in a dropper-bottle), and then, as the crowd which gathered under the shelter had become so tight-packed that communication by gesture was no longer possible and only the voice could be used, he switched to politics (Nixon's gone, the rain's come!). There were also two dark-haired gipsy girls, wearing a motley of colours over their dark-flowered skirts, freshly washed, ironed and starched; local people called them simply 'the blacks'; all night they sat out on a bench in the park that ran down from the graveyard, close to the Day-and-Night sausage-stall; according to a pure-blonde local girl they were only out to trick people and steal from them, though there was no evident justification for her saying so. The crowd also included the owner of the five-roomed hotel – wearing a narrow-brimmed hat – and a very young soldier with a red silk scarf round his unbelievably thin neck. All *travellers* now were gathered under the plastic corrugations of the bus-shelter roof. GRIEF AND HOPE.

The young man who had imitated the firing of the shots in the direction of the monument had been previously explaining something at great length to professor Tashkalidze.

'Understand?' he would ask from time to time.

'No, I don't. *Ei ymmärrä,*' Tashkalidze confessed, for he really could not claim to know Finnish.

But the Marksman was not disconcerted in the least. Without even bothering to observe the customary requirement of a brief introductory silence, or even a fractional check in lieu of a pause, he launched straight into his recital, letting rip as soon as Tashkalidze had nodded to show that the place on the bench beside him was free and had gathered up his papers to make room.

The Marksman rattled on. During his tirade he kept pointing at the rows of red stones, hardly larger than 20 cm^2, that marked the soldiers' graves. The marble stones sloped backwards, with a drop of only 3-4 cm from the head of the stone to the ground. Behind each was a small geranium bush, but the flowers had not been arranged with the same regularity as the grave-stones and, seen from above, would probably have seemed to be no more than trifling details among the rows of stones which (again probably) would have appeared like scales on the back of some prehistoric monster.

Not knowing Finnish, Tashkalidze did his best to pick out the simplest ritual gestures from the long words and cling to them for support as a possible means of later breaking his way into the monologue. And so now, as a tentative gesture of response, he pointed behind them to a gravestone, one and a half metres high, in traditional style, bearing the inscription in Swedish:

FREDERIKA SAVANDER

Föd 17 1 92   Töd 18 15 74

7   8

Professor Tashkalidze had been pondering over this for several days. He was amused by this absolutely realistic way of recording time, which, by means of a graphical device, had succeeded in overthrowing the surrealistic domination of a two-dimensional concept of time, in that the months and days were recorded not *before* the year 1792 but *in* it. In this conceit he discovered a child-like mischievousness, a sprightliness of mind, as though someone had been playing hide-and-seek with the constraints of the two-dimensional perception and communication of reality, and hence of paper.

Had the Marksman realised that the professor's gesture was not directed so much at the large grey grave-stone itself as at the mischievous mockery of the surrealistic representation of reality to which we have become accustomed, he might perhaps have been more appreciative. As it was, however, he indicated in no uncertain terms that he did not approve of Tashkalidze's efforts at communication, since to him the several hundred little red marble stones and Mrs Savanders's tombstone were incomparable and diametrically opposed phenomena.

It is possible that the fresh dawn air was not a good catalyser for conversation (though it was damp – and water is an excellent conductor of currents). One can, for instance, carry one's voice across a river from one bank to another by bending down to the surface of the water, which carries in itself and is by its nature able to encompass all the forms and rhythms of the universe, transmitting the power that radiates from our hands and the instructions of the planets, so that through the water content of our bodies we are guided along secret itineraries known only to the leaves and the stars.

The Anatolian conversation also took place beside a river. Tashkalidze and his fellow archaeologists had been excavating among the cupola-shaped hills, covered with sparse grass* During one of the lunch-breaks, when they had already reached the watermelon-stage, they realised that they were being observed by a Turkish family of about ten members, including a dog, which was the first to approach Tashkalidze's team in order to sniff around among the leftovers. The dog was followed by the father

---

*The excavations did not meet with the anticipated success, as the expedition discovered only a few metal axes. Nevertheless, it was here that professor Tashkalidze was inspired to write the famous study in which he so brilliantly argued that these barren cupola-shaped hills may have served as a model for the turban worn by the Turks during their wars of invasion.

and the grandfather. The father seized the dog by the scruff
of the neck and, with the grandfather's approval, whirled it
into the river as a punishment for its intrusive curiosity.
After this, the father and grandfather settled down beside
the archaeologists, leaving behind their women and
children. After a few dumb gestures of refusal, they
accepted the watermelon and then bawled out for a little
boy, who promptly appeared with tobacco wrapped in
scraps of faded newspaper.**

The grandfather offered tobacco all round; then the
whole family approached (one woman hanging onto the ear
of the sodden dog, which continued to whimper at her
side). The remainder of the watermelon was now
consumed, and the father launched into his story. It must
have been about 40°C out there, and the wilting willows on
the river bank were giving less and less shade. For a while,
it seemed as though the father's words were actually
materialising and being stacked side-by-side in the air
above the archaeologists' heads, adding fractionally to the
earthward-striving weight of the air, sagging lower and
lower, like washing on an overburdened clothes-line, soon
to descend upon the members of the expedition and dissolve
into drops of water on their foreheads. Or perhaps, if the
archaeologists had already continued on their way, they
would have reached the earth and trickled away among the
grass-stems.

Everything, however, was altered by professor
Tashkalidze's behaviour. Instead of calmly surveying the
words of the Turk evaporating in the vector currents, he
stood up before them, attempting to arrest their movement
by picking out one or two sounds which he was able to
distinguish individually and repeating them with frequent
nods of reassurance.

This apparent resistance only stirred the Turk to fiercer

**The print was no longer legible, but Tashkalidze was
nevertheless able to establish that the newspaper was not
Turkish.

efforts, and his words rebounded like hard rubber balls, glancing off in all directions from the hermeneutic wall of professor Tashkalidze's conceptions.

He may have been talking about huge birds swishing through the air, or else about aeroplanes, and, as a consequence of this aerial commotion, the Turk went on to relate an instance of death, graphically illustrating – by sawing at his neck with an outstretched hand – the decapitation. The incident most probably occurred in some distant place, far from the family's mud hut, the road, the turban-shaped hills, and even – in all likelihood – the Aegean Sea.

When he came to indicate the place where this incident had occurred, the Turk became still more passionate and vehement, and there was much shaking of fists; then, with Professor Tashkalidze's grinning connivance they repeated over and over again two words which must surely have meant that somehow they had managed to outwit the distant enemy.

It seemed that a repetition of the story now ensued, and Tashkalidze was growing more and more confident in his ability to understand the words, though every now and then he was thrown out of his stride by the introduction of a new development. The Turk showed no signs of slackening down, indeed, his narration took on an added intensity. Making vehement gestures towards the river he returned time after time in an ever-diminishing spiral to the focal point of his tale – the decapitation. Then suddenly he jabbed sharply with one hand towards the river and the other towards the hills, his body serving as a link between the two gesticulatory limbs while his face reflected a passionate expectancy. But cracks were fending the defensive wall of Tashkalidze's comprehension and the Turk's faith in his companion was rapidly crumbling, so that soon they were left facing each other blankly again as two strangers.

It was then that Tashkalidze's brainwave occurred. He took out a ballpoint from the left pocket of his shirt, and, having no other paper to hand, tore out a page from NIN (*Nedeljne Informativne Novine* – a weekly news magazine), and proffered it to the Turk, indicating that he should use it to give an illustrated version of his story. After a moment of silent concentration, the Turkish father set to work, guiding the pen with slow careful strokes so that the pictures would fit into the clear margin without running into the print: he drew two ducks, one after the other, then with shining eyes showed it round, first to Tashkalidze then to the other members of the team.

Tashkalidze silently shook the Turk's hand and posed for his photograph to be taken, first with the Turk, then with the whole family, and finally with all his companions crowding in as well. Then the Turks left, followed shortly by the archaeologists.

Professor Tashkalidze was not inclined to offer the Finnish Marksman the same opportunity of giving pictorial expression to his words, for he doubted that the constantly threshing hand would be capable of drawing a steady line. The Marksman was wearing a grey checked suit, under which he had a dress-shirt, flaring out into ruffles at the end of the – somewhat too long – sleeves. At his neck – a bow-tie. For a long time, Tashkalidze concentrated exclusively on the scything motions of the hands; later he even blocked his ears as well so that Marksman's words should not disturb the rhythm he was trying to discern. In these movements, he fancied he had discovered some pattern, and the gesticulations no longer struck him as being nervous, merely hasty. Moreover, the wide white sleeves stretched out in front of his eyes put him in mind of the benediction.

'So much to bless and so little time to do it in,' the scholar noted to himself.

Some time later, the frilly white shirtsleeves began to droop, and Tashkalidze once again riveted his attention on the words. VEERA, VEERA, the Marksman repeated several times, after which it was clear that what he had in mind was the VEERA restaurant, of which the neon sign was visible from the cemetery.

It also became evident that the Marksman had just come from the VEERA, where he and professor Tashkalidze may well have seen each other. The scholar even took out of his pocket the VEERA INTIIMI-RAVINTOLA – a green matchbox (even the sides were green, but with black spots on which the yellow matches were struck). The Marksman nodded vigorously to indicate his recognition. He said he had been drinking milk and vodka with beer chasers. It was now the teacher's turn to nod, for he recalled having seen this combination drunk at several tables. At one table, a group of Finns had even remarked that 'vodka and milk is our white liquid gold,'* after which Tashkalidze mentioned a photo-reportage in which hops were referred to as 'our green gold',* and a newspaper article with a headline describing the sea as blue gold for bathing tourists. Tashkalidze was fond of such comparisons and, as he observed in one of his well-known studies, 'gold as a basic standard in the measurement of values has played, and still plays, a generally progressive role in the weakening of imperialism.'** It is worth mentioning that in this work Tashkalidze speaks most positively of the late French President De Gaulle, who had also attempted to restore the importance of yellow gold and re-establish its role vis-à-vis the green dollar in international monetary transactions. Tashkalidze stressed that certain concepts (e.g. the dollar and gold) were of necessity turned into symbols and watersheds.

*In speaking of our green gold, this reportage laid particular stress on the fact that 'it now depends on the deftness of our nimble-fingered women and the far-sightedness of the directors of our hop-combines whether or not the crop can be laid in before the heavy rains.'
**See Tashkalidze: Gold as a basic standard of value in progressive rhetoric. Rhetorical Gazette, January 1970, p.168. 'Every adherence to or deliberate rejection of which will strengthen or weaken, respectively, the movement itself, and in the final analysis strengthen or weaken imperialism.'

This is why one should not be tempted to consider that some regrettable technical hitch has occurred in our social lives when such notions or words begin to be formed as are deemed good or bad independent of their context. Objectively speaking – Tashkalidze asserted – there do exist good or bad words and concepts.

The professor had repeated these ideas in the VEERA, adding that he could not but rejoice at the heady progress of gold's career as a metaphor. He also drew the attention of those present to the fact that in his home country, maize had been described in the press as 'yellow gold', and thus the circle had been closed.

During the course of this improvised lecture, Tashkalidze noted with satisfaction that the music in no way interfered with what he was saying, for he found it soothing rather than aggressive. Instead of pulverising his thoughts it pillowed them. YMMÄRTÄÄ – I UNDERSTAND, the male-singer's voice repeated over and over through the loudspeaker. A lanky dancer, with plastered-down slicked-back hair, who was performing the tango with scythe-like but pathetic movements, from time to time passionately clutching then kissing the neck of his great lump of a partner, nodded whenever the singer reached another YMMÄRTÄÄ. Several couples were dancing among the tables. The windows were draped with velvet curtains, on account of which the lights had to be switched on even at lunch-time.

One of the waitresses (wearing a black knitted top and a skirt of the same green as the match-box) sat down at Aari Karvonnen's table. Aari had the biggest biceps in the VEERA, one might have thought the biggest in the whole land, even beyond it as well. Everyone knew that Aari had been a seaman: he had spent 15 years sailing the Indochina Sea and the Malay Archipelago, and it was during these voyages that he had lost the use of his right eye. Karvonnen told everyone that he drank only gin, because it was a protection against malaria. Sitting at this table was another Finn, a young worker, in a blue flower-patterned shirt, who

had left his fiancée at home because she was still a minor
and would not be allowed in, and a Dutch musician whom
Karvonnen addressed as the maestro.

'Your jobs,' said Aari, 'are truly international because
they touch all men. Morse and music – these two.'

They all examined the balustrade-like row of wooden
bars whose real function may have been (or should have
been, said the musician) to separate this room from
another. The bars, however, had been set right up against
the wall, so that it looked as if two cardboard blocks had
been set next to one another. Or as if it were some kind of
Baroque swimming-pool, designed by captain Nemo, out of
which the water had been drained. It seemed almost as
though the lanky dancer felt this lack of water, for in his
movements he seemed to be seeking some kind of liquid
resistance. Most likely, he would have been the only one to
stay on his feet if water had suddenly begun to pour in
through the kitchen door and the ventilation outlet.

Tashkalidze first registered the Baroque-like carved
columns as an architectural oddity. All this, he felt, must
have had some connection with the wooden-handled door
he had seen on a narrow bridge at the Persian border.

The expedition had even stopped to examine the bridge,
but they had been disturbed in their investigations by a
Persian lorry-driver who drew up beside them and switched
on his radio full-blast so that they should all hear a song
called SHIRAZ. The members of the expedition politely
listened through to the end, but when a new song started up
they all turned back towards the bridge and indicated that
this was what interested them.

The driver obligingly ran over and opened the door,
ushering them in ahead. The archaeologists crossed over
the fast-flowing stream and looked back as the driver set off
in his lorry which was spangled and studded with lamps of
all colours and cats'-eyes – one of those lorries which, if you
meet it at night, baffles you completely because you can't
tell whether it's coming towards you or going away.

During the break between the two dances, Tashkalidze

stood up, crossed to the table opposite, and, excusing himself to the group of young men who happened to be drinking vodka with milk (and beer-chasers), began fingering the carved woodwork of the wooden bars and the wall behind them as well. (It is quite possible that the Marksman was one of this group of young men.) But since he did not observe anything special, he went back to Karvonnen and asked a question – one of those which, while he was still busy making preparations for the trip, he had decided must at all costs be broached.

'What is your opinion of Finnish architecture?' (Tashkalidze did not mention the bridge with the door, but he hoped that a spontaneous answer to this – perhaps at first, irrelevant-sounding question, might throw some light on the matter of the bridge-door as well.)

In answering, Karvonnen said – as was only to be expected – since, after concluding his career as a sailor and marrying, he had entered the building trade:

'The most important thing is that we never waste plaster. If, for instance, we were to build a wall across the courtyard, we wouldn't make it straight but indented, with three-sided right-angled detours round the trees. (Conservation of the environment or Umweltschutz, as the Germans call it.) Then in the evening we'd plant fast-growing grass seeds in the ground which had been prepared during the day, and we'd take a shower using the old-fashioned stove and water-heater which had been taken out of the bathroom right at the beginning of the year. (The water would be heated by solar energy, though we could always light the stove if necessary. And the water spraying from the shower and splashing off our bodies will be a great help to the freshly-planted grass.) Let's say, that in the afternoon one of us mixes more mortar than is needed: we can't let it stand till the next day because by then it'll have hardened, and we can't pour it away, either, because that would be a waste. If there's no other solution, it's still best to put a double layer on the bricks. At any rate, what matters most is not to waste mortar.'

Everyone agreed.

For the first time, now, Tashkalidze began to apprehend the connection.

The Marksman did not spend too long with the Veera Intiimi-ravintola matchbox; his attention soon wandered back to the gravestones. He got up from the bench, went over to the nearest marble stone, crouched down, and stroked it repeatedly. (No doubt to get the truest possible sense of its proportions.) Then, standing in front of the professor, with the fine grey dust originating from the body of some fallen hero wafting like incense smoke from his flared shirt-sleeves, he plunged into his explanation.

After fixing the teacher with a short intense stare, the Marksman turned back again towards the gravestones, ran in front of one row and back again, describing a straight line in the air with his index finger parallel to the marble stones. After this, he set off again, angrily, this time running upwards alongside the gravestones, then pounding round the back

They passed no more than one or two cars during their drive from the door-bridge to the border. From time to time they came across a herd of goats but saw no signs of a settlement. The young shepherd boys who had been pelting them with stones as they passed, now also appeared less often, and they no longer had to keep swerving the Combi. Very occasionally, a stone would strike the bodywork like a huge night-beetle. One of the members of the expedition recited The Nurse's Song (Innocence), then they all sang. Night was drawing in.

After the last stone had rebounded off the roof of the car, they all realised that it was indeed the last. It cut through the silence like a snapping guitar-string. Between here and the border they met only the beggar with the incense. He stood in the road like a lame ghost in his white 'shador' (from which, as Tashkalidze later demonstrated, our and down the other side and along the front to complete the rectangle. He came to a stand-still, panting, in front of the professor, and spread his arms out wide to demonstrate the senselessness of the whole lay-out.

The Marksman now returned to his place on the bench and continued with his monologue, speaking far more calmly than before. He explained THE ALTERNATIVE.

It was somewhat easier now to keep track of what he was saying (at least, this was professor Tashkalidze's impression). At any rate, his opening statement sounded like this: The shape of reality is not rectangular!

'The shape of reality is not rectangular,' the Marksman repeated, then he went on: 'If it were rectangular, then the number of fallen heroes would always have to be an even number. We cannot allow ourselves to become enslaved by such pre-formed concepts. Concepts, anyway, are always misleading – as in football for instance. The

word 'shelter' is derived). Unlike the Marksman, he did not have ruffles at the wrists of his white linen sleeves. When the Combi stopped, the beggar leant in at the window holding a smoking tin can, which he swung like a thurifer to bless the occupants. He accepted without a smile the Persian 5 *rial* piece, then stood back to let the expedition continue on its way. The archaeologists tried to guess where he was going to secrete the small metal coin. Tashkalidze's suggestion was that he probably heated a piece of wire in the glowing coals of his incense-can and used this to bore a hole through the coin, which he then threaded onto a cord woven from the pliant stems of roadside bushes and hung with the others over his chest. (The Persian 5 is like an inverted heart).

At the Turkish border the customs officers quickly dispensed with the formalities. On this occasion they were not even interested to know if the archaeologists were carrying tea, as they had done when the expedition crossed the newspapers go on and on about the importance of this tactic or that concept and about how much it matters who is going to dominate the centre-field or who is going to force the tempo of the game. During training sessions, the members of the reserve team are given the task of imitating, for instance, the Brazilian team's style of play. Thus, the goalkeeper is expected to imitate Leao's defence tactics so that his team can learn how to shoot goals at the real Leao – as if the Brazilian goalkeeper were merely a style to be studied, a conception of the game and not a reality. This, of course, is all done on account of the trainers and some of the managers, because if it were really the conceptions that decided everything, it is they – and not the players – that would be in the limelight. In reality, however, everything depends on whether the ball is shot straight in or a few centimetres to the wrong side of the goal-post. Look at the results – there's the proof! 2:1 – the Germans scored twice, the Dutch only border on entering the country. The members of the team were a little disappointed by this for, as great tea-lovers, they were always glad to have tea, even if only as a topic of discussion. Persia was separated from Turkey by a wooden fence with a two-winged gate which was closed by a padlock. When the gate was opened, two planks, like projecting eye-teeth, gouged ruts in the ground. The gate opened towards Persia. The expedition's Combi was the only vehicle in the Persian customs enclosure. First, the passports were checked in a room where the windows were plastered with the corpses of mosquitoes and other winged creatures that had come to a sticky end on the panes. The effect was that of a car's windscreen after a long night drive. Though these streaks and smears were not the traces of a sudden dizzying death at an unnatural speed but rather the cumulative record of days and weeks of methodical work by deft fingers rendered supple by much probing and prodding once. And this might easily have been the reverse, as far as the conception was concerned. Reality is not rectangular in shape – not nowadays, at any rate. It may have been so in some primordial time beyond our ken when the first steps were taken to organise and ritualise reality, starting probably with the Question. The Question – but not in the sense of a sudden peek at the Unknown, a fissure appearing without warning in the secure wall around us, but rather as a wonderful device to conjure up familiar and cherished responses. Like the expectation of a loud report when you place a succulent leaf over the hole formed between your thumb and index-finger and slap it with your other hand. Making human communication more like nature, changing events into rules and patterns. In those times, wit served essentially to decorate the path from question to expected answer – as in the works of our distinguished social scientists, who have not only ready questions but ready answers as well, and excel in for heroin among nuts and bolts, here descending with a practised forehand ease to darken the window-panes. A young police-officer, barely 20 years old, examined the passports at great length and with evident interest, and then, having thumbed through them, slowly set about making marks in them. He then informed the archaeologists that they would have to wait for the customs inspection. The police officer now took up an illustrated magazine to put in some serious reading while Tashkalidze and his colleagues waited. Half an hour must have passed before Tashkalidze, with outstretched hands, asked what had happened to the customs officers. The young man signalled to him to be patient. When, half an hour later, Tashkalidze asked for the fourth time with evident impatience what was going on, the officer left the room and walked over to the fence. They all followed him. On the other side of the fence, the Turkish officers and their Persian guests were having dinner at a long adorning the link between them with the flowers of their precious punditry. Eruditon comes up with brilliant reasons for claiming the established answer to be most appropriate to the present problem. Our happy grin is a Pavlovian reminder of the joy of the Question-Reaction ritual.

Rectangularity may have been passed down to us as some kind of abstract embellishment like, for instance, the abstract reliefs on ceramic dishes, which are themselves an imitation of the reality of the wicker basket – the vessel which preceded the ceramic dish and served a similar function. This inheritance could not simply be disregarded. We are loath to give up the concept of the wicker basket; we would like somehow to retain it, even though its function as a dish has long since vanished. Through clinging to the heritage of the past, conservation leads to abstraction and ornamentation.

But our ambition now is to be progressive! We want reality! Well, if that's what

table. The officer called for Ali, Mirzah, and Hussein, then made a sign to the archaeologists to indicate that everything would be all right, although Tashkalidze might have placed a very different interpretation on the guarded gesture – internationally considered as unequivocal – made by the three Persians. Another hour and a half passed. The team had now taken several turns round the yard, with which they had become more than familiar, and it struck them that they had the numerical superiority. After vehement protests, the officer went to waken one of the customs officers who was supposed to come on duty only at midnight. The pyjama-clad officer was about to launch into a lengthy speech, but when he realised that nobody could follow a word he said, he contracted his message to a single question: Boom-boom? Tashkalidze understood that he was interested in arms, and shook his head: No boom-boom. And when the customs-officer nodded to indicate that they might we want, we should not for instance place the gravestones in neat rectangular rows, but have them scattered like fragments of windscreen at the crossroads. And all around them there should be chalk-white flowers. A rectangle cannot contain and control both grief and hope. Though, come to think of it, perhaps it would be best if the grave-stones were strewn about like soldiers after they've been shot.

continue on their way, he repeated once again: No BOOM-BOOM.

POOM + POOM

POOM-BOOM, POOM-BOOM, the punchlines are loud reports.

LAST MOVEMENT

It must have been about half an hour to the start of the meeting. Strezovski and Yomtobian were already hard at it in the conference-hall, their words ping-ponging round the empty room, rolling down the corridor and round the whole building without meeting any opposition save the occasional dripping tap. Their voices, however, could not escape past the entrance-door because, although the porter had left his booth and was strolling round the building, he had left his transistor-radio playing on the table and the blaring folk-music barricaded the doorway, holding back the intelligence which might otherwise have leaked out.

Outside, around the building, the ground had dried up following the afternoon rains, and the ridges of the dark mud-streaks were beginning to lighten. The porter was filling his lungs with deep breaths, pausing from time to time to gaze through his green-tinted sunglasses (which it would have been embarassing to ask him to return now that the painting was finished – indeed, such a request might even have aroused suspicion), at the site where ten years ago building had been interrupted, leaving only four concrete pillars standing with thin reinforcement bars drooping down; then he let his glance travel further, across the road and over to the stand of the football-stadium opposite, then round and back towards the town, over the low buildings, right up to the tall tower of the Post Office.

'I'm looking through my sunglasses,' the porter said to himself, and he was convinced that his act of looking round would acquire the fullest significance if he were to let his

eyes carry to the farthest possible point in whichever
direction he looked. Like this, he felt, he was also gaining a
reprieve. On turning left, his glance was suddenly arrested
for he found himself standing scarcely a metre and a half
from the wall of the building. Behind the ground-floor
windows lay the conference-hall. Only fragments of the
discussion between Strezovski and Yomtobian could be
heard:

... it is high time ... without undue optimism or undue
pessimism ...

... rumours are circulating that ...

... personally, I have no ...

... and last of all I should just ...

... because if we set out from here ... we could join Weber
in saying ... let's say, for instance, that the indicators for
fish-economy ... at all events, it is worth calling attention
to ...

... taken by itself alone ... cannot be separated ... on the
other hand, mere mechanical combination ... it isn't the
form that really matters ...

... I'm no believer in strong-arm tactics ... not
administrative measures, of course, but ... because from a
different angle ... this does not necessarily mean that ... to
put it briefly ... if, however, we consider that ...

Although Strezovski and Yomtobian were alone in the
room, their remarks, even in this disjuncted and
fragmentary form, were not without connection with a
greater logical, coherent and unified pattern. A chance
bypasser, unacquainted with the particular measures
adopted by the Committee, according to which Strezovski
and Yomtobian were instructed to start half an hour earlier
– measures which were affected on the one hand by the
debaters' notoriously detailed and circumstantial way of
reasoning, and on the other hand by the requirements of
efficiency and democracy – might have thought he was
listening to a rehearsal by the leaders of a declamation
chorus.

At any rate, it was in the air that something was brewing,
taking shape.

Tsu Tao, Kismárton and Scattone were the first to appear on the road leading from town towards the building. Tsu Tao was telling them about his reactionary grandfather who spent 7-8 hours a day listening in to all imaginable short-wave broadcasts:

tu-tuuu- tu-tuuuu
   beep-beep
tu-tuuu- tuuuu
the English are coming
we'll get back our factory.

When they reached the porter – who had meanwhile returned to his booth – Tsu Tao once again let out his:

tu-tuuu- tu-tuuuu
   beep-beep
tuuuu-tuuuu-tuuuu
the English are coming
we'll get back our factory.

The porter greeted them.

Kismárton asked if anyone else had arrived yet. When they learnt that only Yomtobian and Strezovski were in the hall, they decided it might be better to wait for the others in front of the building.

Soon a large group arrived comprising: Vargas, Lawrence, Durrell, Horváth, Butor, Theo, Rogers, and Jovan K. Milošević. At the entrance, everyone shook hands with everyone else, then, for Tsu Tao's sake, Rogers went right back to the beginning of a joke he had already half-told on the way.

'An American, a Luxemburger, and a Zairean were travelling by train together. They were disputing over which country had the toughest yarn. In the end, it turned out that the yarn from Zaire was the most resistant.'

Then Durrell and Kismárton each told a joke involving an American, a Luxemburger and a Zairean.

The joke-telling was still under way when Balogi, Kappengut(h), Hjalmarsson and others arrived.

It was already five o'clock, and those attending the meeting were still standing around in the street, perhaps even intentionally postponing the event. The porter – whose fashionable green glasses may have influenced his impression – saw clearly that they were all delaying.

Balogi was first to take the plunge. The neon lights had been switched on in the entrance hall, but for the moment they merely tinted the daylight entering through the wide glass doors. The oblong hall was divided into six parts by pairs of columns; from the side it looked like a hall for a ping-pong competition.

The last opportunity for delay occurred at the end of the hall, beside the last column on the left. They all turned their backs to the staircase, which began a few metres away, faced round towards the entrance again, clustered in a semi-circle round the column and began to study the programme affixed to it. Kappengut(h) read aloud:

FESTIVAL PROGRAMME

1. Opening address (guest)
2. Opening address (host)
3. Johann Wolfgang von Goethe: Der Erlkönig, poetry recital
4. Franz Lehar: My heart's love, song recital
5. Johann Strauss: Waltz – orchestral recital
6. William Blake: Songs of Innocence (The Nurse's Song), poetry recital
7. Folk dances – dance performance

INTERMISSION – FIFTEEN MINUTES

8. Shakespeare: The Merchant of Venice, excerpts from the play
9. Schubert: Serenade, piano recital
10. Mazisi Kunene: Universal love, poetry recital
11. Alan Jay Lerner: On the street where she lives, song recital
12. Emery Kálman: The Gipsy Queen (operetta), excerpts
13. Sandor Petöfi: Hang the kings, poetry recital
14. Folk dances – dance performance

When Kappengut(h) had finished, utter silence fell. The porter had already switched off his radio, and just at that moment (or perhaps while the programme was still being read) Yomtobian and Strezovski broke off their discussion. This sudden hiatus – like a 'break' in jazz, as Hjalmarsson would have said – helped to re-establish, even intensify the expectancy aroused by the thought of the forthcoming event.

All the way up to the conference-hall (from in front of which the empty paint tins had been cleared away) there were no more exchanges of opinion. Lawrence merely remarked to the centre-half, who had caught up with the others on the steps, that his back hurt him all the time. The centre-half politely replied that he too suffered from back-ache.

'Whose back doesn't hurt nowadays!' ... Arak added resignedly.

Once they were inside, gathered around the oval table and the DURALEX glasses, the customary self-conscious joking for some reason was not to be heard. It may have been because it was already almost a quarter past five, but more likely because the tension of expectancy was gaining an ever stronger hold over those present. When Ms Margit finally arrived, somebody did remark that she must have been overdoing the siesta, but nobody said: 'here's the quorum' when the sixty-year-oldish man in spectacles and a beret arrived.

And when Vargas read out the proposed agenda, all that could be heard was the flickering of the neon lights.

Then Kavanomoku stood up to put *the question* in the form of a proposition:

BEFORE TURNING TO THE MISCELLANEOUS QUESTIONS WE SHOULD, I BELIEVE, DISCUSS AS A SPECIAL ITEM ON THE DAY'S AGENDA THE MATTER OF WHY THE CONFERENCE-HALL HAD TO BE PAINTED MOUSE-GREY, OF ALL COLOURS.

REPRISE

'It's not what he said, but the way he said it.'

'Yes, because if he had just simply said I've no right to go on holiday twice a year, that would have been different.'

'Quite different.'

'But it was the way he said it. The way. Otherwise I wouldn't have had any objections. It could even have been regarded as a matter for consideration amongst comrades.'

'But his way of …'

'It was the way he …'

'I mean, if he had just …'

'Nobody would have had the slightest objection. I'd be the first to shake hands with anyone who honestly criticised me.'

'But this clearly can't be allowed to go on.'

'Like last time, with Svatopluk. If he'd only just said simply that overtime can only be considered as work performed outside of working hours, we wouldn't have said a thing.'

'But the way he said it! And he even wanted to make it into a special item on the agenda.'

'Sheer exhibitionism.'

'Because I wouldn't have had the slightest objection if …'

'But the way he …'